Information and technology in the supply chain

e-supply chain: revolution or e-volution?

Welcome to

NEW YORK

PARIS

While you're considering the impact of eBusiness

In case you haven't noticed, your customers—especially Web customers—aren't very good at waiting.

As the world's leading provider of supply chain management and Intelligent eBusiness solutions, we at i2 Technologies can help your enterprise make the critical link between what your Web site promises and what your supply chain is able to deliver. After all, the key to eBusiness success is a well-managed supply chain, delivering exactly what customers want, exactly when they want it.

USA: 214.860.6000
Europe: +44.1628.601.200
Asia Pacific: +65.339.6000

Internet Time.

TOKYO

INTERNET

ur business, how long will your customers wait?

Our customers don't like waiting either.

More than 700 i2 customers worldwide aren't making their customers wait. Our supply chain and eBusiness solutions are designed to be implemented quickly— delivering immediate results. Which gives our customers a dramatic competitive advantage. Now doesn't that sound like something you've been waiting for?

To find out more, call us to get your free copy of the "Intelligent eBusiness" white paper, or simply download it from our Web site at www.i2.com.

Our two most important pie

s of equipment.

e*Gate

ERP

BANK

VENDORS

WAREHOUSE

DISTRIBUTION

560 STORES

SUPPLY CHAIN SYSTEMS

PricewaterhouseCoopers (www.pwcglobal.com) is the world's leading professional services organisation. Drawing on the knowledge and skills of 155,000 people in 150 countries, we help our clients solve complex business problems and measurably enhance their ability to build value, manage risk and improve performance.

PricewaterhouseCoopers refers to the member firms of the worldwide PricewaterhouseCoopers organisation.

© Euromoney Institutional Investor PLC

Published by
Euromoney Institutional Investor PLC
Nestor House, Playhouse Yard
London EC4V 5EX
Tel +44 (0)207 779 8888

Publisher: Roger Davies
Advertising manager: Angus Chapman
Advertising executives: Debbie Ormonde, Puneet Veerma
Sub-editor: Michael Halls
Production editor: Norma Ewart

Editorial board: Rob Garratt, Richard Powell, Jeremy Robinson and Mark Yeomans.
Authors: David Dockray, Matthew Faulkner, Nick Ford, Rob Garratt, John Kamauff, Andrew Jackson, Melissa Marroso, Nick Miller, Conrad Nowikow, Ray Powell, Richard Powell, Jim Tizzard, Alan Waller and Mark Yeomans.

ISBN: 185564 795 8

Printed and typeset in the UK by The Manson Group

The information contained in this publication should not be relied on as professional advice and should not be regarded as a substitute for detailed advice in individual cases. No responsibility for any loss occasioned to any person acting or refraining from action as a result of material in this publication is accepted by the editors, authors or publishers. If advice concerning individual problems or other expert assistance is required, the service of a competent professional adviser should be sought. The opinions presented by the individual authors do not necessarily reflect the opinions of PricewaterhouseCoopers.

Is supply chain management a fad?

Well it's a fad saving us $75 million a year.

Every month you hear the hype on supply chain management (SCM). How it will make you more flexible. How it will speed your time to market. And how SCM will save your business money. But where's the proof?

Well try this: through implementing SCM, Cisco achieves $75 million in savings including labour, indirect and direct costs every year. We have generated over $100 million in revenue annually due to faster time-to-volume for new products. And we've reduced our customer order cycle from 6-8 weeks to an average of 1-3 weeks.

While the pundits spread the hype, we're making it happen. To find out how we could help you make SCM a reality, visit us at www.cisco.com

CISCO SYSTEMS

EMPOWERING THE
INTERNET GENERATION℠

WHEREVER PEOPLE DO BUSINESS, THERE IS EQUANT.

48.8° Latitude

2.3° Longitude

©1999 EQUANT International

Paris 3:17 p.m.

Your largest customer wants to do e-business. He says he needs more information. What he really needs is insight and expertise. Is the market viable? Can he count on local support? Can he get the right application? Can it be integrated with his supply chain management apps? He needs answers. He needs Equant. Only Equant combines a network reaching over 220 countries and territories with a global team of application and integration experts to tackle the most complex IP-based business solutions. Owning and operating the largest private network on earth is just the beginning of Equant's reach. Deregulation, global expansion and e-business are part of life. Isn't it nice to know Equant has you and the world covered.

www.equant.com

Americas +1 888 731 3100   Europe +44 (0) 181 321 4000
Asia Pacific +65 332 9288

EQUANT

Contents

I know which buttons to push.

{ The ones that give me access to all your confidential files. }

N
e
t
T
o
o
l
s

Dr Solomon's/McAfee
Total Virus Defense

PGP Total Network Security

Sniffer Total Network Visibility

Magic Total Service Desk

SHE'S THREE KEYSTROKES AWAY FROM BRINGING YOUR NETWORK TO ITS KNEES. UNLESS, OF COURSE, YOU'RE PART OF THE 80% OF THE GLOBAL 1000 WHO HAVE CHOSEN NETWORK ASSOCIATES FOR THEIR NETWORK SECURITY AND MANAGEMENT. IF SO, BREATHE EASY. IF NOT, IT'S PROBABLY NOT HER LOOKS GIVING YOU SHORTNESS OF BREATH. TO FIND OUT MORE ABOUT NETWORK PROTECTION, AND A COMPREHENSIVE INFORMATION PACK ON NETWORK ASSOCIATES FAX +44 (0)1753 827434, OR VISIT WWW.NAI.COM. OK, NOW EXHALE.

network
ASSOCIATES™
Who's watching your network

Foreword

As we enter a different millennium, a new phenomenon is changing the way we do business. Electronic trading has been around for a while, in one guise or another, but technology advances have opened it up to the mass market and given it more power. The growth explosion has started and is set to continue.

Electronic commerce is getting a lot of publicity, but will it really affect us the way the hype suggests?

To help answer this question, I am delighted to introduce the 2000 PricewaterhouseCoopers guide to e-business, and its impact on the supply chain.

In this book, we examine the key e-business issues that will face businesses and senior management over the coming years. We discuss the changes in consumer buying patterns and their impact on distribution networks, manufacturing and procurement. We describe the supporting technology, its impact on knowledge management and communication between businesses. We look at the commercial pressure for even more efficiency in supply chains, and the methods that might achieve it.

This guide has been prepared by experienced consultants from many sector backgrounds. They have helped design the supply chain strategies of many of the world's leading organisations and have shared in their subsequent implementation. The book presents their knowledge of what really works and the foresight generated by their breadth of experience.

At PricewaterhouseCoopers, we make a real difference to our clients by addressing issues that affect the whole of their business to achieve excellence. In this way, we improve our clients' value, competitiveness and capabilities — in short, their success.

Will e-business be a revolution for the success of your organisation? I hope this book helps you decide.

Yours sincerely,

David Dockray
Global Leader of Consulting Services
Commercial and Industrial Products Sector
PricewaterhouseCoopers +44 (0) 207 583 5000

auer, Compaq, Office Depot, Tower Records, jcpenney.com, Universal Stud
ds.com, barnesandnoble.com, American Diabetes Association, pcflowers.cc
Magenic.com, BestBuy.com, Costco.com, toysmart.com, British Telecom
Force Exchange Service, Harvard Business School Publishing, Wizards of th
QVC, SkyMall.com, www.bombayco.com, Peet's Coffee & Tea, MasterCard, M
hopping.com, PCMall.com, Ron Jon Surf Shop, randmcnallystore.com, GreenGr
Starbucks.com, Growl Bear Outfitters, Godiva.com, Adaptec Global Services

W
Fro
or C
ente
inte
e-cc

© 1999
† Inform

Microsoft®

Where do you want to go today?®

Online Store & Auction, Spiegel.com, Staples.com, StockPoint.com, Buy.c
ioneer Electronics, TrinityZone.com, GlobalProShop.com, John Deere-Home
ntmall.com, FoxHome.com, PetExpress.com, CDW.com, AtYourOffice.co
ast, Orvis.com, WineAccess.com, Oregon Public Broadcasting, CompUSA.co
Fool's FoolMart, OnSafari.com, www.levi.com, www.dockers.com, Pitney-Bow
.com.au, Forbes, WineAccess.com, albertsons.com, Cooking.com, LA County, Fo
erican Health Network (AHN), visio.com, BuyBroadway.com, Software Spectr

is list has yet to reach an end, it all starts with a Microsoft® e-commerce solution.
Kids.com to Retired Persons, Inc., more decision makers consider Microsoft a strategic e-commerce partner than IBM, Sun, Netscape,
fact, companies from all industries are adding their names to this list every day, whether they're small businesses or billion-dollar
whether they're implementing value chain integration or putting their stores in touch with customers. Quick, easy deployment,
y with a diverse set of existing systems, and easy access to online services are just a few of the ways that Microsoft is enabling
or everyone. To find out how you can benefit from a Microsoft-based e-commerce solution, visit www.microsoft.com/dns

Executive summary

This book assesses the impact of e-business on the supply chain, both within an organisation and between its trading partners. It presents a vision of the near future, and shows how companies can manœuvre now to make the most of the new business environment, optimising their efforts and capitalising on the potential offered by emerging technologies.

We are being bombarded with signs that the e-business age is upon us. The popular media see this embodied by the Internet, which provides a new channel to market for retailers.

The truth is more pronounced. This channel provides the potential to by-pass the retailer altogether and offer direct consumer access to the manufacturer or brand owner. In some areas, such as branded fashion goods, this is already happening.

The Internet alone does not constitute the e-business revolution, but it is a major driving force behind the shift in business focus towards the consumer. The new market is a consumer-centric one, in which trading partners are brought together at just the right time to produce goods and services tailored to individual requirements.

The Internet provides access to the mass consumer market, and the potential to understand, record and influence individuals' buying profiles.

The power in this new environment will lie with the controllers of the consumer profiles. Traditional retailer influence is under threat, as they will no longer be the sole representatives of the consumer in the supply chain.

All businesses, whatever their role in the supply chain, will need to relate to consumers, managing relationships as their key competitive asset. They will need to exploit technology as it advances, and rework their processes to fit the new business model. Agility and flexibility will be the differentiators, and organisations will need to be even more efficient to make their business pay.

Business-to-consumer is not the only area being redefined. The pervasive nature and efficiency of electronic commerce will affect the routine transactions between business partners. Many believe the most immediate impacts will be in business-to-business transactions. The conversion of many routine transactions, from purchasing, designing and planning to e-purchasing, e-designing and e-planning, will stimulate profound organisational changes.

The Internet is the catalyst, but it needs a supporting cast of technology and innovative processes to make the new model work.

Agility needs flexible manufacturing, with large batch sizes making way for shorter runs of a wider range of products. The tailoring of products and services to an individual customer or consumer brings into question the location of the inventory, and where secondary finishing takes place.

To increase efficiency, purchasing of materials must be established as an integral part of the new product development cycle and the purchasing of non-production items offers huge opportunities for savings through electronic cataloguing and information management.

The role of logistics service providers is changing as they share information and move closer to their customers' core supply chain. The anticipated increase in consumer-direct deliveries, and even more responsive business-to-business needs, will re-shape the service they provide.

New technologies can make the supply chain transparent, enabling all elements to see the true demand. To be an effective player in the market, an organisation will have to invest in the technology that gives access to that information and to manage the knowledge it generates. It must also invest in the applications software that makes use of the information, such as planning and scheduling systems, and begin the process of optimising the supply chain.

The enabling technologies of e-business are continuously evolving, but their application across the supply chain is triggering a fundamental change in the business models of all organisations.

Of the Fortune 500 companies, 68% say that the cultural resistance of staff and management is the biggest hurdle they face to implementing technology. The electronic supply chain is not just about technological change — it is about cultural change in management policies, performance metrics, business processes and organisational structure.

The e-supply chain of the future will be wrought with change and challenge as every company in every industry is affected by the disruptive forces at hand. The stakes are high, and the rewards vast.

The challenge to compete is before us all, and the only way to compete in the future is to define it.

OVERVIEW

This book is written by PricewaterhouseCoopers' most senior practitioners. Our aim is to share with you the understanding and insights developed both from our independent analysis and our experience of working every day with the world's best organisations.

The book is divided into 13 chapters.

Chapter 1: The challenge

This establishes the vision for e-business over the next five years, discussing recent technology and e-supply chain developments and the likely trends and issues to be faced by organisations as they come to terms with the new ways of doing business.

Chapter 2: The future in chains — the view from the bridge

This looks at e-business trends and defines the function and purpose of a supply chain in the new environment.

Chapter 3: The consumer-centric supply chain

This presents a vision for the future that is totally consumer-focused, and discusses the impact of that on the supply chains of consumer packaged goods companies.

Chapter 4: Selling in cyberspace — the brave new world of retailing

A description of the effects of e-business on retailing, and the impact on existing retail distribution networks.

Chapter 5: Acting with agility — creating the e-factory

This discusses the response of manufacturing to the pressures created by a consumer-focused supply chain.

Chapter 6: Living with the enemy — working with service partners

This describes the changing scope of the logistics service providers as the traditional supply chain continues to evolve.

Chapter 7: Creating virtual advantage — planning the optimised supply chain

This chapter takes the service level and effectiveness trends and reviews the opportunities for dynamically optimising supply chains, including the use of advanced planning tools.

Chapter 8: Sourcing for support — e-procurement

An examination of the opportunities for the procurement of non-production goods and services, including the development of electronic catalogues.

Chapter 9: Sourcing for production — e-design

This demonstrates the advantages of Web-enabled information sharing during the development of new products, to optimise the sourcing of purchased components and materials.

Chapter 10: E-essentials — the technology that drives the change

This looks at the technology developments that are making the changes possible, including hardware and software standards, methods for the integration of e-commerce tools with legacy business systems, and the important issues of personalisation and security.

Chapter 11: Harnessing the power of knowledge

A discussion on the importance of harnessing the knowledge that the new systems and processes will generate, and describes tools to help manage it.

Chapter 12: Organising for the future

This describes the effect of the changing environment on the organisation itself, and the business's response to it.

Chapter 13: Revolution or e-volution?

This presents a view on whether e-business will bring about a revolution, or merely an evolutionary change, within the supply chain. It summarises the challenges facing tomorrow's business leaders.

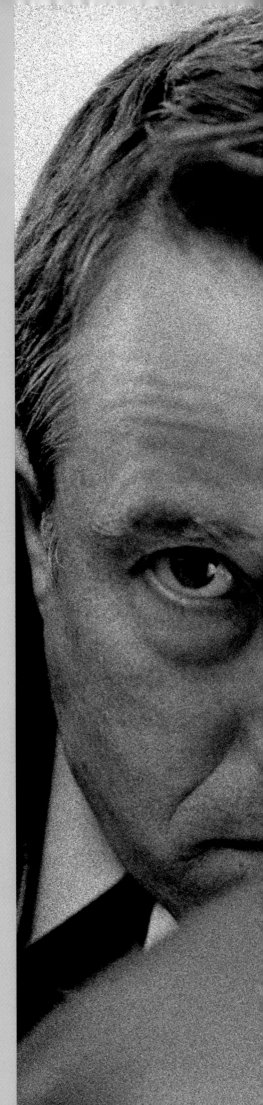

Allow us to summarize this book.
Business as usual is over. Mourn quickly.
The task at hand is to prepare the enterprise
to operate in an environment wherein almost
all business relationships will be driven by the
online infrastructure – a phenomenon which
raises the enterprise transformation stakes
to the moon once again. Going forward,
your ability to compete is clearly tied to your
ability to evolve – continually improving
business processes at the speed of changing
market conditions and customers' demands.

How do you run a business this way?
As you might suspect, we have written the
software to accomplish it forthrightly.
Intense, but eminently doable.
Bring your business strategies online
with speed and a new level of flexibility.
Join the Movement. Contact Jackie Davidson.
jackied@interworld.com
InterWorld Corporation 44 1753 708 618

Please visit our web site for a
complete list of worldwide offices.
www.interworld.com

INTERWORLD®

Leading The Enterprise Commerce Movement

The power of technology.
The power of understanding. The power of Chase.

**A more powerful platform for success:
Chase E-business Solutions**

At Chase we go beyond traditional banking to provide the best electronic solutions—that don't merely solve problems. They anticipate your future needs as well.

We combine our proven technological expertise with an in-depth understanding of our clients to create a powerful array of web-based products and services. As one of the first to recognize and harness the potential of web technology, we're helping our clients enhance their overall performance.

We continue to be at the forefront of creating web-based solutions that enable you to achieve your goals more effectively than ever before. Which means you'll have even more ways to maximize your returns.

For further information, contact Raymond Fattell at
Raymond.W.Fattell@Chase.com

 **CHASE**

THE RIGHT RELATIONSHIP IS EVERYTHING.®

www.chase.com

The challenge

INTRODUCTION

Companies are missing major cost savings and revenue opportunities by focusing on retail applications of e-business rather than the improvements that an integrated electronic supply chain can bring to day-to-day enterprise-wide operations.

Yet, according to Forrester Research, 68% of Fortune 500 companies believe cultural resistance of staff and management is the biggest hurdle to implementing technology, and 58% think internal groups represent the biggest challenge to supply chain partner collaboration.

In this environment, it is imperative to remember that electronic-supply chain management (e-SCM) is not about technology change — it is about cultural change in management policies, performance metrics, business processes, and organisational structure across the value chain.

E-business, which started as a new way of co-ordinating transactions more efficiently via the Web, has evolved to become a general principle for organising production and exchange across the enterprise-wide supply chain.

When properly planned and executed, e-SCM presents organisations with a chance to achieve strategic superiority, create global sales and service opportunities, strengthen trading partner relationships, streamline the supply chain, enhance operational efficiencies and effectiveness, reduce transactional and overhead costs, and optimise human resource usage.

Dyed-in-the-wool technophiles may know that the first commercial Internet, called Telenet, was unveiled in 1974, but many CEOs and practitioners have only recently and reluctantly been dragged into the technologically-enabled Information Age.

Now the ever-pervasive Internet seems to be at the core of every business discussion, or, as it has come to be known, the foundation of everyone's e-business. And despite the insistence of Luddites that "no one's making any money in the e-space", everyone else seems to be betting their future that they will.

In 1996, just 16 million computers were connected to the World Wide Web. In 2000 it will have topped a quarter of a billion. The Internet is radically changing society and business — in ways that we have only begun to explore. Physical distance becomes irrelevant, and waiting time for information access and transactional execution is only a vague memory.

E-business can be defined as the application of information technologies to facilitate the buying and selling of products, services, and information over public standards-based networks. The key here is the term "public", which replaces previous forms of electronic data and information interchange over dedicated or private networks.

E-business extends beyond traditional e-commerce as much more than just a new Web site on the Internet. It goes far beyond new technologies to impact all aspects of an organisation from strategy, process, organisation and systems, to its trading partners and the ultimate consumer.

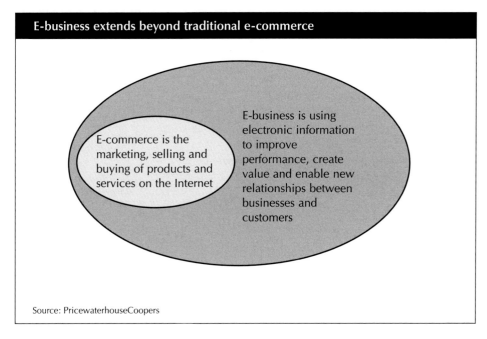

E-business extends beyond traditional e-commerce

E-commerce is the marketing, selling and buying of products and services on the Internet

E-business is using electronic information to improve performance, create value and enable new relationships between businesses and customers

Source: PricewaterhouseCoopers

Much of the initial emphasis on e-business has been on the 'e' rather than the 'business'. The focus of this book is to put the business, particularly business-to-business connectivity, back into e-business, and specifically into e-supply chain management, in addressing the untapped potential that exists.

E-business is an inherently disruptive market force. The survivors will overcome it; the visionaries will exploit it.

Ten predictions for the e-commerce age

E-business versus e-commerce	The benefits of doing business electronically will attract increasing interest as companies realise the importance of not merely doing business better but doing business differently.
Business solutions, not technology products	The realisation that a successful e-business is more about business than technology will continue to grow.
Senior management on board	E-business is moving into the corporate boardroom with its promise to build business. CEOs will find themselves managing a regrouping of company functions in response to increasingly flexible information and distribution channels and the disassembly of the value chain.
WWW achieves true global status	There will be exponential growth in the number of Internet users. This will be linked to the increasing globalisation of business as the Internet removes geographic boundaries.
Customer is number 1	Corporate e-business initiatives are accelerating the move of global business to consumer-centric organisations.
Security and privacy first among equals	E-business security and privacy are critical to success in attracting new online business.
Role models wanted	Companies want to see more successful e-business examples before embarking on such endeavours themselves. As the body of knowledge and experience grows, so will the use of e-business. Role models are likely to come from information-based industries such as financial services, advertising, publishing and high-tech.
Partnerships	Effective partnerships will be one manifestation of the highly networked organisational model of the future. They will cause companies to re-assess their core and non-core competencies.
Investments	E-business will continue to be a"net cash out" proposition in the short term as companies build in the infrastructures needed to succeed. The emergence of additional solutions packages and experienced implementers will lessen the risk involved and ultimately lower support costs.
Taking the plunge	Companies will greatly expand their investment in e-business systems. There will be a rapid growth of e-business for both front-end and back-end operations, with the separation between the two continuing to narrow.

TRADEXPRESS
Advanced Electronic Commerce Software

EVERY BUSINESS NEEDS
ELECTRONIC COMMERCE

Electronic commerce is transforming the face of today's business. In an expanding global marketplace businesses are presented with exciting new opportunities and sources of profit. New challenges and demands exist, all of which must be answered.

In the world of business to business electronic commerce every company is unique. Each has its own set of applications and finance systems, infrastructures, partners, and customers. The electronic commerce solution should therefore also be unique. It should also be flexible enough to incorporate today's architecture yet provide a scalable, easy, and reliable transition to tomorrow's standards.

Sonera TradeXpress is the solution of choice. It is a robust and scalable software platform on which your company can reliably build an electronic commerce solution that fits perfectly.

Sonera TradeXpress is designed for mission critical, event-driven transactions and has a fast high-volume throughput suitable for even the most demanding environment.

Unique business rules can be applied to each individual transaction making it the most accurate, secure and reliable electronic commerce tool available today.

Sonera TradeXpress is a platform for developing the secure and reliable electronic commerce solution your company deserves. Sonera TradeXpress is also an excellent choice for business to consumer back-office connectivity.

Sonera TradeXpress will take you and your business successfully into the 21st century.

http://www.sonera.fi/tradexpress

E-BUSINESS OPPORTUNITIES AND THREATS

If organisations can capture and use the potential of e-business, they will achieve competitive advantage. This potential exists despite an era of globalisation, regulation and constant technological change that make it ever more difficult to increase profitability and shareholder value.

E-business adaptors will win the loyalty of consumers, customers and suppliers alike who, driven by the Internet, are redefining buying and selling patterns and are forcing businesses to reformulate strategies to leverage the power of the next generation of information technologies.

E-business has the ability to create dramatic new sources of shareholder value by enabling organisations to accomplish the following goals.
- Build customer loyalty.
- Reach new markets.
- Create new products and services.
- Achieve market leadership.
- Optimise business processes.
- Enhance human capital.
- Harness technology.
- Manage risk and compliance.

However, as shown by the rapid ascendance of amazon.com and Dell to leadership in their respective industries, e-business also puts some companies and, in fact, entire industries at risk.

What keeps CEOs awake at night is concern over which company will be the next Dell. Moreover, many of the most successful traditional companies are those that are the most vulnerable. Strategy and plans are transparent to competitors and latent competitors — those challengers who were never even envisaged are the most threatening. Barriers to entry are diminished.

Competitive advantage is short-lived; and an ever increasing need to create products and services with partners prevails — the ability to ramp up or ramp down quickly may be the only remaining short-term competitive advantage.

E-BUSINESS AND e-SCM

E-business

Most of the initial flurry of activity around e-business has focused on the business-to-consumer aspects of the Internet. However, this focus has shifted with $7.5 billion of $9 billion on-line transactions in 1997 being business-to-business sales.

The focus on e-business emanates from intimate customer and consumer relationships. It is derived from a hitherto untapped capability to:
- Develop and deliver products and services faster.
- Extend geographical reach.
- Increase process efficiency and effectiveness.
- Redefine products, services and brands.
- Leverage information by providing more flexible infrastructures and business models.

Electronic supply chain management

At its most basic level, e-SCM addresses this notion of using information technology to conduct seamless and virtual business transactions among buyers, sellers and trading partners.

The technology is used to improve customer service, reduce costs, and increase shareholder value across and beyond the enterprise through the streamlining and customisation of the value chain buy-sell process.

At its core, e-SCM, with its inherent emphasis on people, process and technology provides the technology-enabled backbone for business-to-business relationships. These ultimately build, enable and deliver what the Internet promises.

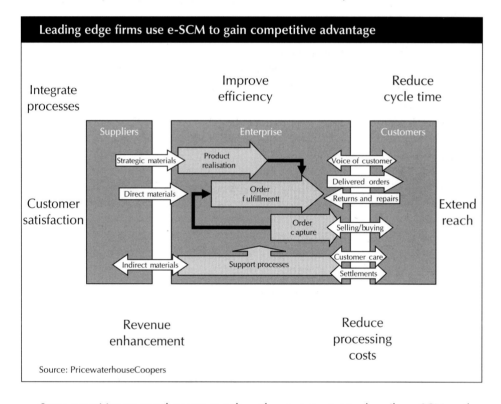

Source: PricewaterhouseCoopers

Some practitioners use the term supply web management to describe e-SCM as the process of co-ordinating and managing the interactions between businesses to meet the end customer's requirements. Developing and using cheap and reliable communication media such as the Internet can facilitate information sharing.

To some extent, e-SCM means building the links (both literally and figuratively) within and between organisations across the enterprise, from suppliers' suppliers to customers' customers and ultimately with consumers. Technically speaking, it involves taking processes currently functioning within businesses and moving them to networks and shared applications.

Like e-business, e-SCM has been built on technology but, unlike electronic commerce, its ascendancy is less about technology than it is about business.

It is about satisfying individual customer and consumer needs. Ultimate success will be enabled by the technology, not caused by it. It is about connecting supply chains to enhance communications, collaboration and customer service. It is about doing business differently, being acutely aware of a new range of options that are becoming available to survive, compete and succeed. In the final analysis, e-SCM, building upon the Internet and the disruptive nature of associated technologies will affect everything about the way people operate across the enterprise and will profoundly affect both our businesses and our lives.

E-BUSINESS — WHAT'S DIFFERENT: THE IMPLICATIONS OF INFORMATION BROKERAGE

Minimal standardisation, the existing infrastructure and technology base, population density and economics have resulted in the co-existence of localised networks using leased lines, virtual private networks (VPNs) and the Internet, employing different architectures and technologies.

The ability to integrate these technologies will enable businesses to seamlessly operate globally. Applications and e-business models will drive the demand for more bandwidth, speed, security, and a higher quality of service, which will itself drive the demand for VPNs, dedicated connectivity solutions, and network architectures that can meet these needs.

Manufacturers and service providers, availing themselves of this transformation, are trying to reach the consumer directly and also then integrating that information directly into their operations.

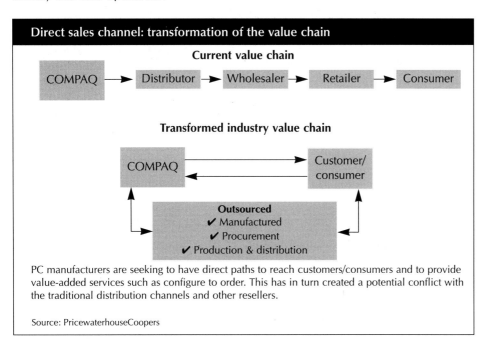

Direct sales channel: transformation of the value chain

Current value chain

COMPAQ → Distributor → Wholesaler → Retailer → Consumer

Transformed industry value chain

COMPAQ ⟷ Customer/consumer

Outsourced
✔ Manufactured
✔ Procurement
✔ Production & distribution

PC manufacturers are seeking to have direct paths to reach customers/consumers and to provide value-added services such as configure to order. This has in turn created a potential conflict with the traditional distribution channels and other resellers.

Source: PricewaterhouseCoopers

In this context, connectivity rules:
- The key to the liberating power of any network is the potential it carries for total connectivity.
- Every increase in connectivity creates an increase in value — sometimes dubbed "the law of plenitude" — because of the enhanced synergistic effect of greater information flow.
- Knowledge workers and information brokers will prevail.
- To paraphrase Metcalf's Law (in itself a modern version of the old law of increasing

returns), the value of a supply chain increases in direct proportion to the square of the number of partners that are on it.

E-business is concerned with the impact that connectivity has on customers and suppliers. Connectivity is the key, particularly as it applies to business-to-business integration.

Few can discount that the prevailing sense of prosperity that predominates in the Western world can be attributed to the productivity gains and technological advancements of the past several decades, yet CEOs themselves are demanding more. They need to maximise their technology investments and, in particular, their enterprise resource planning (ERP) systems.

E-business and, specifically, e-SCM, with its focus on increasing the number of supply chain partners connected to one another, offers the next exponential productivity opportunity.

In this context, information brokerage — the ability to assimilate, synthesise and use information to satisfy business solutions — becomes the barometer of success. And the future is predicated upon having effective people — knowledge workers — who can enter information quickly into databases, integrate e-SCM software into existing on-line systems, and, even more importantly, synthesise the information in a way that allows real-time decision making.

E-SCM — THE FOUR-BOX MODEL

For most organisations, e-SCM takes place within the four phases of a company's e-business:

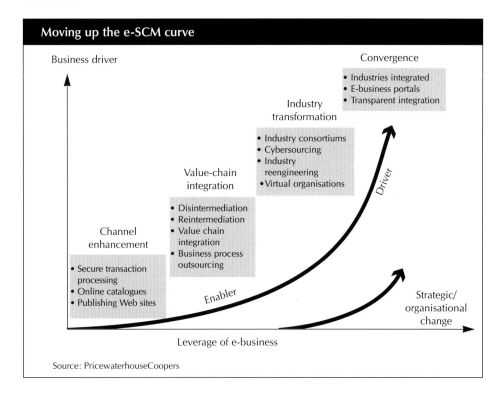

Moving up the e-SCM curve

Source: PricewaterhouseCoopers

- Channel enhancement
- Value chain integration
- Industry transformation
- Convergence

Although one does not necessarily mature through the phases as sequential stages, the first two deal primarily with changes to existing business models whereas the latter two encompass major transformation of the business models as well as to the industries themselves.

Channel enhancement

Channel enhancement focuses on generating demand for retail consumers and business customers.

The intent is to use the Web to extend customer reach using on-line pages of product information, while establishing new ordering channels and creating point solutions using e-business to automate existing business processes. Frequently, the goal is to deepen penetration and reach and boost service or product mix.

For example, Eastman Kodak has used the Internet to extend its services beyond processing film. Once consumers have digitised their photos, they can use the Kodak Website to order reprints and enlargements, provide friends and relatives with access to their on-line photos and use on-line tools to enhance the pictures, for example by removing red-eye, or adjusting the colour balance.

Peapod, a US home-delivery grocery service, now provides a 24-hour fresh produce delivery service and has used the Internet to increase the ease with which customers can place orders. More importantly, it gives customers the ability to schedule their delivery, selecting time slots that are available for their area.

Managing demand over the Internet brings challenges that exacerbate the issues facing existing global business models. Direct interaction with consumers forces sellers to become externally focused and, as barriers to entry fall and more competitors enter, sellers will focus on relationships as the foundation for subsequent lifetime sales.

Ultimately, however, consumers will take charge of the entire process and dictate their own individual and often unique value proposition. As consumers become overwhelmed with the wide variety of offerings, sellers will necessarily compete on lowering the overall buyers' cost — the total cost of ownership. This scenario, if played out, can only be addressed by overcoming value chain limitations and exploiting the opportunities of the enterprise-wide, electronically enabled supply chain.

Still, channel enhancement has other challenges, such as in understanding and addressing channel conflict. An investigation into, and resolution of, potential channel strategies should precede all e-SCM initiatives.

Issues that must be addressed include: cannibalisation of existing channels; how to reward staff; how to equate prices; and, how to deal with volume or product mix decreases in physical stores while handling similar (or hopefully greater) increases in alternative channels. Other opportunities for enhancing channels allow companies to skip extra distribution steps and move directly to the consumer, as Dell and amazon.com have done. These include:

Customer care: customer-interfacing processes to target, reach, understand, and retain customers.

Are you an automotive manufacturer who wants to deliver product faster or a winery who wants to sell one case at a time?

Microsoft has e-commerce solutions for any business. As companies like Barnes & Noble, Inc. and E-Stamp have already discovered, e-commerce isn't just for businesses who want to sell over the Web. It's for any business that wants to do things smarter. Like respond to market changes faster. Or work better with customers. Or lower costs. By building on existing technologies, Microsoft and our partners have helped thousands of companies create e-commerce solutions for everyday business. To see examples of how e-commerce solutions have helped other companies, go to **www.microsoft.com/go/business**

Microsoft
Where do you want to go today?®

E-commerce solutions for any business.   Microsoft **Office**   Microsoft **Windows**   Microsoft **BackOffice**

Customer order management: order and replenishment processes with the direct consumers.

Channel strategy: new distribution streams leading to increased revenues and new markets — cell phones, interactive TVs, retail kiosks.

Supply chain replenishment: production and distribution strategy using real-time demand and strategic partner alignment to improve consumer responsiveness.

Customer product configuration: real-time, on-line configuration, validation, and pricing of products based on customised requirements to modularise product and reduce engineering costs.

Undoubtedly, these types of solutions have immediate benefits but may not position enterprises to compete in the e-world.

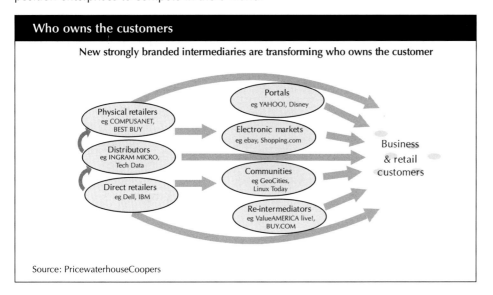

Who owns the customers

New strongly branded intermediaries are transforming who owns the customer

Source: PricewaterhouseCoopers

Value chain integration

Value chain integration (VCI) connects an enterprise with its network of suppliers and customers. It requires connecting the point solutions and new channels across the enterprise-wide value chain and integrating them with the order fulfilment process.

VCI is where most companies are pursuing opportunities today. According to Forrester Research, more than 70% of companies will be sharing demand, inventory and order status by 2001. At the core of this integration is information visibility and access. More important, though, will be the inherent capability of the enterprise to share and use this information in real time.

As an example, Unipart leveraged its EDI networks and legacy systems, and relationships with distributors, to sell directly to customers without increasing order-processing costs. Customers are able to locate the required product from a range of over 20,000 items, check its availability and have it delivered within 24 hours.

Partners with ERP investments are particularly well suited to leverage these technological investments to achieve true value chain integration.

The ultimate goal is to co-ordinate data gathered from customers, employees, suppliers, and even competitors with internal, mission-critical corporate data. Just as importantly, enterprises have to be able to configure and manufacture (or service) to order.

In essence, value chain integration entails real time matching of supply and demand.

Chapter 1

Value chain integration: matching supply and demand

Characteristics
- Fluid flow of information
- Standardised technologies linking disparate enterprises
- Flexible partnerships

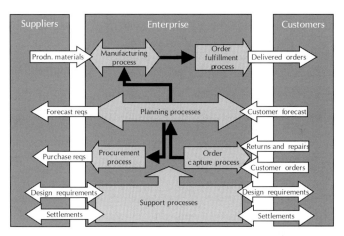

ERP-to-ERP   ERP-to-ERP

Benefits
- Inventory visibility across the supply chain
- Real-time demand visibility
- Real time propagation of supply chain changes
- Seamless integration/relationships with supply chain partners
- Real-time available-to-promise

Enabled processes
- Collaborative forecasting
- E-procurement
- Online order status/tracking
- Pull based delivery mechanism

Source: PricewaterhouseCoopers

Visibility enables firms to move from reactive to proactive supply chains. Most practitioners have always known that this level of enterprise-wide value chain integration was where they wanted to be. Now e-SCM enables it.

Value chain integration areas include the following:

- **E-Procurement**: procurement processes among multiple enterprises using electronic business, eg on-line catalogues, auctions, and exchanges.
- **Component and supplier management:** the design and implementation of product design and supplier integration into the product development process.
- **E-logistics:** warehouse and transportation management processes using electronic business as a means of increasing value, eg vendor managed inventory, hazardous materials, and import/export.
- **Supply chain tax and legal alignment:** the analysis and implementation of tax and legal recommendations, aligned with global and virtual supply chains.
- **Differentiating value chain strategy:** the development and planning of new business models that provide competitive advantage through e-business.
- **E-trading:** the use of auctions, aggregates, and exchanges across the value chain to reduce obsolescence, product costs, and inventory investment.
- **E-factory:** the integration of real-time information to maintain planning and control across the virtual supply chain.

- **Collaborative planning:** the redesign and implementation of planning processes across multiple enterprises, using electronic business to synchronise product flow, optimise resource allocation, and reduce inventory.
- **Product data management:** the redesign and implementation of product design to manufacturing processes to minimise costs.

Industry transformation

Most organisations initially pursue value chain integration with an eye towards industry transformation — which is ultimately the alteration of the successful business model. In this context, the emphasis is on core competencies, those activities that customers and consumers value and will pay for.

Necessarily, processes are disaggregated and taken over by specialists. Dis-intermediation and re-intermediation prevail, speed of reaction rules and electronic connectivity makes this far easier.

Companies in this phase re-evaluate their core strengths to determine how they can dynamically balance supply with demand. Those activities that keep them from achieving this balance will be outsourced to those who can do it better.

Amazon.com epitomises the concepts of industry transformation. The firm outsources most operations while concentrating on customer relationships.

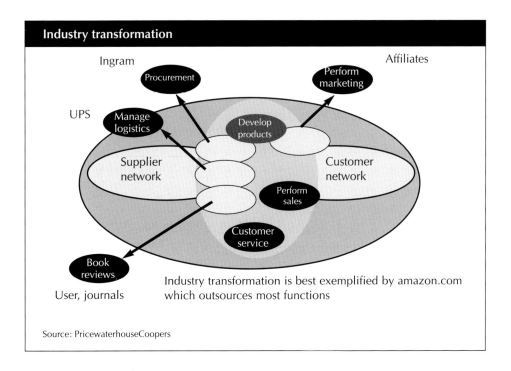

Industry transformation

Industry transformation is best exemplified by amazon.com which outsources most functions

Source: PricewaterhouseCoopers

This move toward core competencies is not without risks. It suggests three e-SCM strategies of the future, all of which are based on mega-processes and are predicated on real-time information brokerage across the enterprise-wide value chain:
- Become intimate with the customer/consumer and deliver products/services with speed and agility.
- Become the efficient and flexible manufacturer and distributor (or service provider).

- Be the product/service leader while matching consumer and customer needs (either consumer/customer-driven 'pull' or enterprise-driven 'push' based on uncovering latent demand).

Cisco has fundamentally changed the nature of the network hardware industry by addressing e-SCM through its innovative applications, many of which the customers did not know they needed or wanted until they had them.

- Technical self-help allows users to answer questions, download software updates/diagnostic tools, and communicate on-line.
- Product configuration allows Cisco to price, configure, and validate orders on-line.
- Software distribution sends upgrades and new releases electronically.
- Collaborative planning enables sharing of incoming orders and forecast changes, makes inventory visible to all supply chain partners, and enables dynamic replenishment.
- Electronic document delivery transmits orders, schedules, and changes on-line.
- Web-enabled product testing allows engineers to manage testing with automated tools.
- Collaborative product development opens communications with suppliers and reduces physical prototypes.

For Cisco and its customers, the results have been outstanding:

- $82 million savings due to reduction in engineers, technicians, and service representatives.
- Order errors decrease from 15% to 2%, lead time shrunk to between two and five days.
- $250 million savings in production and shipping costs.
- $70 million reduction in supply chain costs, including 45% inventory reduction and $35 million in labour avoidance.
- $100 million increase in revenue and $21 million reduction in R&D costs from 25% lead time reduction.
- Reduced order and configuration cycle time by 50% while reducing customer order time by 25%.

Additionally, other industry transformation opportunities include the following.

- Collaborative product development: the design and implementation of product development processes across multiple enterprises using electronic business as an enabler of speed, accuracy, and real-time control to improve product launch success and time-to-market.
- Product life service: the design and implementation of remote product service processes, ie testing, diagnostics, and repair, that can be enabled through electronic business to reduce cost-to-serve and define new revenue streams.
- Knowledge management: the strategy and implementation of capturing, retaining, and retrieving enterprise knowledge to increase corporate learning.
- E-product content: the electronic enhancement or distribution of client product offerings, ie software, using Web-enabled technology.
- Supplies chain reconfiguration: the redesign of processes to enable flexible supply streams to enable responsiveness to new customers and products.
- Third party brokering: the selection and transition of multiple supply chain partners to a new operating model that leverages core competencies and reduces costs.

Convergence

Convergence implies an ability to delve into non-traditional products and services, to break the rules and to establish new business routines.

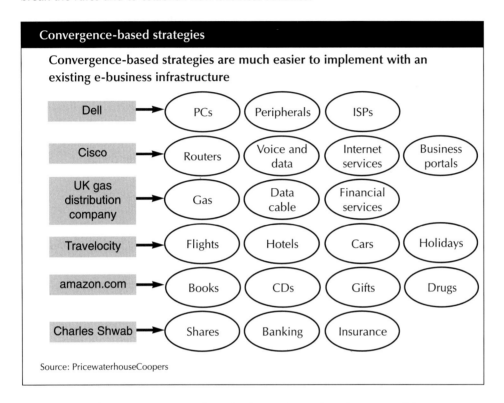

Convergence-based strategies

Convergence-based strategies are much easier to implement with an existing e-business infrastructure

Source: PricewaterhouseCoopers

For example, some CEOs say the rules have changed — the name of the game now is not revenue, but exposure; revenue later, ubiquity first.

Amazon.com and Dell, as well as many other leading retailers, typify the types of enterprises that continue to adopt this strategy. Dell continues to press its advantage, having recently struck a $10 billion deal with IBM for components and technology and having started gigabuys.com, where it is selling components.

Like most companies, convergence implies an ability to move into other retail products. Amazon.com uses e-SCM to provide value-added services, such as new book/music recommendations based on past purchases to build consumer loyalty.

The implication is the emergence of portals that become one-stop shops for consumer or customer needs as they choose the service provider that best serves their overall requirements.

VIRTUAL ORGANISING

In the final analysis, most firms are just testing the waters by implementing point solutions which tackle the issues of only one component of the supply chain. Supply chains of the future will resemble a web with an information pipeline and with infomediaries playing significant roles as advisers, consultants and information brokers.

The enterprise-wide electronic supply chain will be focused on speed, agility and collaboration and will be characterised by customised products and services, global visibility, nimble supply chains, partner leverage and lightning speed.

Using information and flexibly integrated supply chains will enable enterprises to close the loop on their value chains. The virtual supply chain will entail direct-to-consumer marketing and dispatch, based on consumer-centric new product development and real-time usage monitoring.

The closed loop system will also address automatic replenishment, obsolescence, diagnosis and intelligent forecasting.

Product and information will dynamically flow from any node to other nodes in the supply web and all activities across the enterprise will be focused to satisfy the customer's or consumer's individual needs.

Web interfaces will be customised to specific customer needs, with real-time ordering, product information, and dynamic pricing/promotion. On-line what-if configuration of products and services — for example, cars/trucks with personal preferences based on past buying patterns, such as a 50-gallon fuel tank — will be readily available. Configurators will have direct links into manufacturing systems to provide real-time availability to promise. They will rely on inventory visibility and dynamic scheduling across the partner network of supply, operations, and distribution.

Mass customisation will rule, and batch sizes of one (based on the product and service being offered) will become the enterprise norm.

Strategic supply partners will have tightly linked systems. Forecasts will be jointly developed and fulfilled; non-strategic supplies will be captured by way of auctions, aggregates, or exchanges, much like airline tickets can be purchased using priceline.com.

All activities will be focused around delivery of the service to end-consumers, where inventory and order status can be accessed immediately by customers, consumers or trading partners across the Web.

E-logistics will include real-time track-and-trace and visibility into such issues as hazardous materials, import/export and tax advantages.

E-content management will facilitate product and service distribution and updates (eg software distribution and service).

Most enterprises will transform themselves from delivering products to delivering capabilities. They will emphasise product or service perceptions as reality.

In this context, supply web teams will be formed, much like a top sports team, based on tight partnerships — each player has a role to perform on the team, as each partner in the supply web supports the entire delivery system. Players may change periodically, but chemistry between the partnerships is key to success, and supply webs will compete, not companies. Each team will have critical success factors around the ability to build sustainable alliances and partnerships based on enterprise-wide core competencies.

Nimble supply webs will be created and made obsolete on a regular basis. Each partner will maintain a core competency valued by the end consumer (customer knowledge, product design, delivery, and manufacturing) and will leverage the strength of their partners.

Outsourcing of non-core functions will be much easier due to real-time control enabled by e-SCM. Inventory, order, product information, schedules, changes, and performance status will have real-time global visibility.

Above all, velocity across the enterprise-wide value chain will result in decreased supply web cycle time and speed to market for new products and services.

E-SCM IN PRACTICE

Successful electronic supply chain solutions exist today, some of which will be discussed here. However, electronic technology will continue to remain unsettled because of the continuous flow of new products and Web-enabled variants of existing products into the marketplace.

Adaptec

Adaptec designs and builds hardware and software that speed up data transfer between computers, peripherals, and networks. The company sells its host adapters, network interface cards, storage controllers and other systems to Dell, IBM, and other makers of computers and peripherals. With operations in the US, Asia, and Europe and with key suppliers worldwide, Adaptec sought to increase procurement efficiencies. Its key business issues were to decrease supply chain cycle times, reduce inventories, improve end-of-quarter shipments and increase customer satisfaction.

To satisfy these objectives, it adopted an integrated SCM solution approach that included:
- Analysing opportunities for supply chain cycle-time reduction.
- Identifying areas where e-SCM provided the enabling technology to reduce cycle time and inventory across the enterprise.
- Organising integrated, cross-functional teams to include engineering, planning, procurement, inventory control, and suppliers to generate and evaluate the e-SCM solutions.
- Designing an e-SCM solution using Extricity's Alliance software to interface with three key suppliers (TSMC in Taiwan, Seiko in Japan, and ASAT in Hong Kong).

After following this approach, Adaptec's supply chain cycle time was reduced by 50% and it saved $10 million in inventory costs while increasing customer satisfaction levels across the board.

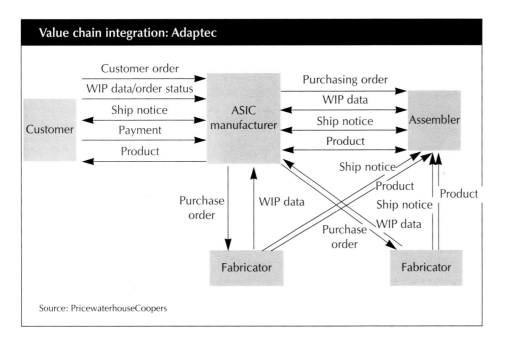

Value chain integration: Adaptec

Source: PricewaterhouseCoopers

Crossing network lines — Thomson Consumer Electronics

It is more than just internal Internets, intranets and extranets that are tying companies together and blurring the boundaries between them. The increasing level of business process integration within enterprises as well as between supply chain partners means that information will be increasingly moving across network lines from intranet to extranet to intranet.

Thomson Consumer Electronics (TCE) is a case in point. TCE invested in an i2 supply chain management system, only to realise that it was not a complete solution for its needs — add-ons such as a sales forecasting ability were needed, requiring new systems of data feeds.

Thomson decided not to solve the problem in-house. Instead it approached a number of technology providers for a solution. The successful candidate was TranSettlements Network Services, an Atlanta-based company that in the 1970s, was one of the early providers of electronic data interchange.

TransSettlements' solution was to develop an extranet accessible by Thomson's customers. TCE's customers log in to their specific area on the system and access a form for each of the products they order. The customer indicates the number of units they will need for each product for each of the next 26 weeks. Customers are also able to go in and change their projections as their requirements change over time, as well as to change a forecast to a firm order.

Once the data is transmitted through the extranet, TranSettlements automatically formats it and uploads it into Thomson's sales forecasting and order processing systems.

Thomson's acquisition of this sales forecasting technology is part of a comprehensive supply chain re-engineering process that the company is undergoing globally.

TCE believes that this has given it a competitive advantage in the marketplace and customer feedback has been positive. The firm is the only consumer products manufacturer that uses projections that the customers supply.

Once loaded into TCE's data warehouse, the information is combined with use history and demand patterns can be analysed.

Since its implementation in August 1998 TCE's extranet strategy has achieved dramatic results including a reduction in inventory levels by $100 million. And because inventory turns have risen from four or five annually to around the eight to 10 range there has been less need to transport parts to manufacturing facilities, giving a saving of between $5 million and $10 million in transportation costs.

Thanks to the smooth flow of data from the extranet into i2, Thomson says it has been able to save on i2 implementation costs of around $100 million to $150 million.

Overall, extranet strategies can be tailored to a wide variety of needs and can be specifically targeted at the virtual community when critical to client service and marketing strategies.

Extranets allow one to tie back to the enterprise-wide value chain from suppliers' suppliers to customers' customers and ultimately to consumers. And the more specific the tie in, the more effective the management of knowledge.

In a world that is made increasingly more virtual, these kinds of strategic alliance both strengthen the ties and blur the lines that determine where one company ends and another begins.

KEY ISSUES FOR THE CEO

- How am I going to incorporate e-SCM as an integral part of my enterprise-wide philosophy?
- How can I use e-business to improve performance and increase value for my shareholders?
- What are the potential opportunities and threats presented by e-business?
- What immediate actions am I going to take to capture the potential that e-business offers to my organisation?
- What can I learn from other organisations in the new e-business environment?

KEY E-SCM CONSIDERATIONS

- E-SCM is business-driven, not an IT initiative.
- Address e-SCM as in integral part of your enterprise-wide philosophy.
- Understand what e-SCM is and how it differs from e-Commerce.
- Understand the total ramification e-SCM can have.
- Tomorrow's business model differs from today's.
- Understand the inherent interdependency of the enterprise in crafting e-SCM initiatives.
- Bandwidth and security will offer hurdles.
- Complete management buy-in must proceed enterprise-wide e-SCM transformation.
- e-SCM is integrative in approach, global in reach and inclusive by nature.
- e-SCM is an evolving area that will require future investment and constant attention to technological, process, and skills developments.
- e-SCM loves rule breakers, but it is important to understand the inherent data access, legal and security issues.
- The name of the game is not revenue but rather exposure — build a name first.
- Things move fast, but do not expect instant profits.
- Winners will master time-tested business principles and cyber rules.

CitiCommerce.com
The new business force

Putting banking into e-commerce. CitiCommerce.com @ www.citicommerce.com is a revolutionary new e-commerce business solution which combines transaction banking services with web-based buying and selling, thus delivering a secure, end-to-end financial solution. CitiCommerce.com has taken cutting-edge technology and added it to the power of the world's leading financial services brand, linking business with financial innovation - to complete your commercial world.

Practical innovations for your company and its customers. Developed with direct input from our customers, CitiCommerce.com offers your company lower sales administration costs, state-of-the-art security and world-class customer service. It has benefits for your customers, too, offering them greater operating efficiency, enhanced information flow and an invoice management system. To see how your business could benefit from this innovative solution, visit our website @ **www.citicommerce.com** .

**BEST CASH MANAGEMENT
BANK IN ASIA***

CORPORATE FINANCE

**TOP BANK IN
GLOBAL CASH MANAGEMENT***

**BEST AT
TRANSACTION SERVICES***

CITIBANK GLOBAL CASH & TRADE

*Awarded in 1997, 1998 and 1999

©1999 Citibank

CITIBANK

The future in chains — the view from the bridge

INTRODUCTION

The traditional supply chain is on borrowed time. It is no longer simply a matter of pushing products and services towards the customer as efficiently as possible. Instead, the supply chain is becoming pivotal to business success and survival.

Best practice in today's supply chain management embraces concepts that would have been regarded as heresy a decade ago. Who would have proposed sharing sensitive demand information with suppliers and creating partnerships with competitors? Frightening as it may seem, the only way to stay competitive in the years to come is to completely redesign the way in which the supply chain operates.

This chapter sets out the supply chain context for the rest of the book by looking at its role within an organisation. Using recent survey data, it reviews the trends that are driving supply chain design and points to opportunities and challenges lying ahead. Driven by these, it summarises 12 imperatives for outstanding supply chain performance.

Across all sectors, companies are extending their geographical reach and influence. Increasing consumer power, economic growth, free trade and rapid advances in technology are all drivers behind the major opportunities for developing business globally. Major new challenges result from the global sourcing of products and raw materials from the best suppliers around the world, as well as the capacity to reach into new markets.

The opportunities are enormous, but, to take advantage of them, companies need to work on turning vision into reality. As the world shrinks, supply chains become longer and more complex. Today's businesses find that the complex corporate supply chains on which they depend stretches across international borders and also embrace relationships with an increasing number of partners and suppliers.

A fundamental reassessment is needed — from raw material sources to final consumer. Businesses must continually synchronise demand along the entire supply chain, working with their partners to optimise the whole, not just the part they own.

The drive for change must come from the top, and the leadership of change needs to be taken up as a boardroom responsibility. Many managers consider the supply chain so crucial to the survival of their businesses that the future has been nicknamed the "supply chain age".

This chapter will identify what businesses need to do to survive in this supply chain age.

THE PWC SURVEY 1998

This chapter draws on research by PricewaterhouseCoopers into the issues facing businesses while they develop and manage cross-border supply chains. The survey, *Shaping the Value Chain for Outstanding Performance* — hereafter called the survey — was undertaken during the summer of 1998.

Its objectives were to determine the key issues driving supply chain development; the competitive forces and trends in supply chain design; and the key enablers and obstacles to globalisation of the supply chain.

Two hundred of the leading European businesses, across 19 countries, were questioned. In addition, extensive interviews were conducted with boardroom executives from 25 of Europe's leading companies. The survey's findings provide a unique snapshot of supply chain drivers in the approach to the millennium and give powerful clues to trends within supply chain thinking.

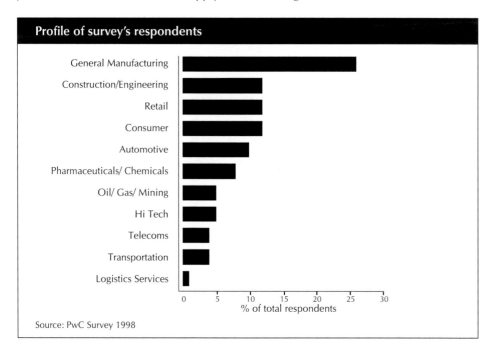

Profile of survey's respondents

Source: PwC Survey 1998

THE SUPPLY CHAIN — DEFINITION

A supply chain is the mechanism that enables products to be available in the right amount, at the right place and at the right time. It covers all the infrastructure, organisation, physical processes and information from raw material to the end consumer. It includes the processes of procurement, manufacturing and distribution, and it needs to operate in a fully integrated way with sales, marketing and new product development.

This means that it must be aligned with busienss strategy and implemented effectively. Both of these are board room responsibilities.

Many companies see supply chain management as a competitive weapon to enhance their position in the marketplace. Their objective is clear — they want to gain competitive advantage by delivering superior customer and economic value, through synchronised management of the flow of physical goods and associated information, from source to consumption.

THE COMPETITIVE ENVIRONMENT — WHAT IS NEW?

So how can the supply chain be used as a competitive weapon?

A first step is to understand the competitive environment in which businesses are operating — and in which the supply chain must excel. The boardroom level interviews in the survey show, without exception, that senior executives acknowledge the importance of improving their supply chain to enhance the competitive position of their companies. External issues are seen as the key drivers behind the need for change. These are grouped as eight global trends that together challenge the existence of today's corporations.

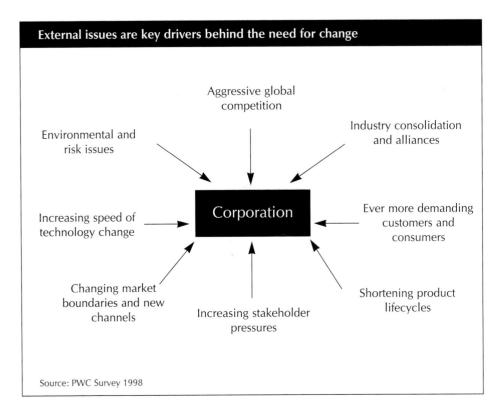

External issues are key drivers behind the need for change

Source: PWC Survey 1998

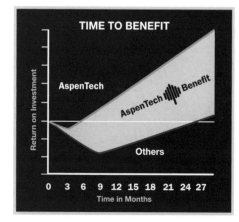

Aggressive global competition

Low cost competition from newly industrialised countries, combined with a reduction in world trade restrictions, present threats in all sectors.

Industry consolidation and alliances

Convergence between sectors, and the increasing number of mergers and acquisitions involving major players, is changing the face of global and local competition.

Ever more demanding customers and consumers

Customers are demanding increased product availability and delivery reliability with greater variety and tailored solutions. In addition, factors such as a single European currency and trading via the Internet enable customers to quickly identify the lowest cost suppliers.

    The largest customers are becoming the most powerful parts of the supply chain. Managing diversity and complexity becomes the reality — and the challenge — within such a customer driven world.

Shortening product lifecycles

Increasing competition is forcing companies to introduce new products ever more rapidly, just to maintain market share.

    This will place increased pressures on supply chains to reduce cost and deliver efficiency — from design all the way through to the physical delivery of products and services to the consumer.

Increasing stakeholder pressures

The business's stakeholders are seeking ever greater returns. Shareholders, analysts, employees and customers are forcing the pace of change. Capital has become more mobile, international take-overs have become the norm, and products must either deliver the return on investment or be killed.

    In this environment, the race for market share and a short product lifecycle is fundamental.

Changing market boundaries and new channels

At the same time as consumers and customers are driving increasing complexity on to the supply chain, new channels and markets are emerging. The ever-widening European single market place, free trade agreements like the North American Free Trade Agreement (NAFTA), together with Internet trading, present radical market opportunities and threats.

Increasing speed of technology change

Nowhere is the speed of change more apparent than within technology. The rapid changes in the power of memory chips, the costs of data storage and the pace at which data networks have been established have resulted in a massive introduction of IT systems and the rapid emergence of e-commerce.

    The information revolution has radically changed the way in which many

The world's fastest-growing ERP solution supplier.

In 1998, IFS' revenues grew by 96 percent. This made us the world's fastest-growing ERP supplier, and one of the ten biggest.

How did we achieve this? A few years ago, IFS pioneered the idea of component-based ERP applications. Instead of huge, monolithic systems that took years to get started, IFS' components could be implemented step by step, and adapt easily to fast-changing business conditions.

Thousands of customers have discovered the benefits IFS' systems deliver. In 1999, we are launching our third generation of component-based applications.

Visit our web site to find out more, or call +44 (0) 1494 428 900.

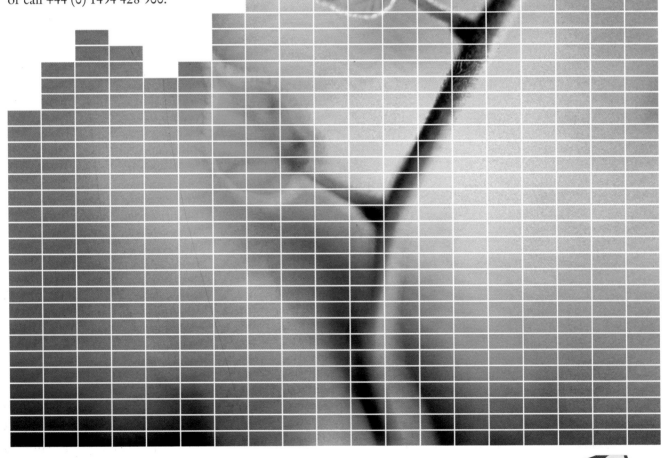

www.ifsab.com

INDUSTRIAL & FINANCIAL SYSTEMS
Set your business free.™

IFS

companies deal with things like routine consumable purchases. IT systems, such as enterprise resource planning (ERP) and advanced planning and scheduling (APS), are vital to remain competitive.

Environmental and risk issues

Increasing legislation on product and packaging recycling, emission taxes and fuel pricing are all beginning to challenge traditional supply chain concepts.

THE IMPACT OF SUPPLY CHAINS ON BUSINESS PERFORMANCE

The survey identified a number of common factors affecting business performance, the top five of which are listed and discussed below.

First factor: increased customer focus

Second factor: supply chain globalisation

Third (equal) factors:

- Reduced time to market
- Strategic purchasing
- Increased supply chain agility/flexibility

The second factor, globalisation, was seen to be predominantly customer-driven. Some two-thirds of the pressures on businesses to globalise their own operations are created by the globalisation of existing customers, new customers in emerging markets, and increasing customer demands. It is evident that the customer is, indeed, the focal point for supply chains of the future.

HOW TO OBTAIN OUTSTANDING SUPPLY CHAIN PERFORMANCE

Once one knows the trends in the competitive business environment, as well as the factors that affect the performance of the supply chain, the concern of senior decision-maker is how to deal with them.

The following key themes emerged from the survey:

- How does one deliver distinctive value and differentiated service to local customers, while at the same time exploiting opportunities from a globalised view of the supply chain?
- How does one align the whole enterprise — people, processes, operations, technology, suppliers, and other business partners — around a programme of progressive strategic change?
- How does one future proof and build agility into supply chain operations in response to the pace of external change and ever increasing pressures from shareholders and competitors?

To address these key themes, 12 imperatives for outstanding supply chain performance were identified. Addressing these is the challenge facing the managers who design and operate supply chains across the world.

The 12 imperatives for outstanding supply chain performance	
How do we deliver distinctive value and differentiated service to local customers, while at the same time exploiting opportunities from a globalised view of the supply chain?	**The strategic imperatives** *Adding value to the customer* **1st imperative:** the customer value driven supply chain **2nd imperative:** differentiation through the product offering *Searching for structural advantage* **3rd Imperative:** global operations restructuring **4th imperative:** strategic sourcing and co-venturing partnerships *Business integration and performance drivers* **5th imperative:** integrating/synchronising the supply chain network **6th imperative:** operations beyond the productivity edge
How do we align the whole enterprise — people, processes, operations, technology, suppliers, and other business partners — around a programme of progressive strategic change?	**The key enablers** **7th imperative:** business structure and organisation **8th imperative:** process and performance measures **9th imperative:** people and behaviours **10th imperative:** high performance partnerships **11th imperative:** leveraging information and technology
How do we future proof, and build agility into, our supply chain operations in response to the pace of external change and ever increasing pressures from shareholders and competitors?	**Managing at the pace of change** **12th imperative:** agility and the ability to respond to change

ADDING VALUE TO THE CUSTOMER

Imperative 1: the customer value driven supply chain

The most important driver of change within today's supply chain is the ongoing requirement to serve ever more demanding customers, both existing and new. External competitive pressures further compound this challenge. The movement from "push/business-driven" to "pull/customer-driven" is a clear trend. Tailored supply chains need to be engineered to meet the needs of different product/service/cost offerings for different customers, channels and products.

Supply chains must be able to handle the demand for consistency in meeting the needs of global customers — but in a way that does not sacrifice local diversity.

The key problem — often termed the global paradox — is how to meet individual customer needs, including local differentiation, local service and local customisation, and at the same time take advantage of the volume economies created by globalisation. Businesses must ensure that every process across the supply chain applies global scale while enabling local responsiveness.

If businesses are to achieve these goals, traditional views of manufacturing need to be abandoned for more creative uses of concepts such as postponement — delaying commitment and tailoring the product downstream, fully exploiting techniques like assembly-to-order. Indeed, businesses must move their manufacturing processes towards design for the supply chain.

Imperative 2: differentiation through the product offering

So how can a company use the supply chain as a competitive weapon to achieve business success?

When asked to identify how businesses could most effectively differentiate themselves against competitors, those in the survey pointed to providing the customer with improved service and value. Traditional differentiators, such as lowest cost, came out with far lower priority in the survey than the customer service elements.

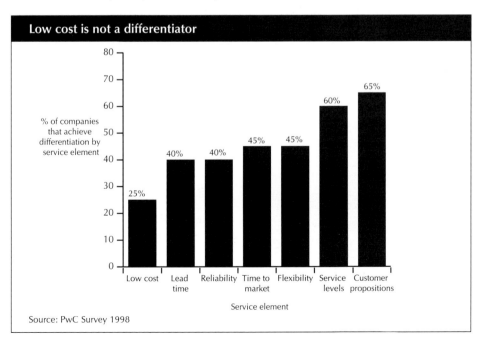

Low cost is not a differentiator

Source: PwC Survey 1998

While the need to unlock the potential of the supply chain is widely recognised, the majority of businesses in the survey were unclear where to start. Even for the most advanced businesses in the survey, the route to reconfiguring the supply chain, to enable the transition from "push" to customer-driven "pull", is not well recognised.

Imperative 3: global operations restructuring

Companies recognise that as their supply chains become longer and more complex, radical restructuring of their supply, manufacturing and distribution components becomes essential to realise volume economies and streamline the route to market.
Some of the big globalisation challenges on the agenda are:

- How best to exploit the potential of e-commerce on a global basis.
- How to restructure the end-to-end supply chain assets, creating extended enterprises using partnerships.
- How to manage increasingly complex programmes.
- How to move to efficient business-to-business trading.

Globalisation is a continuous process, and even the most progressive organisations in the survey recognised they still had a difficult journey ahead to achieve this. Initiatives to globalise processes have to be carried through with care, and a sophisticated model is needed which gains the benefits from globalisation (advantages of core technologies, scale, reach and geography) while still ensuring that the need for local responsiveness is satisfied.

Imperative 4: strategic sourcing and co-venturing partnerships

Globalisation offers opportunities to improve performance and gain competitive advantage from sourcing. There is a clear shift in attitude towards co-operation between businesses — with the survey showing that partnership is seen as the way forward.

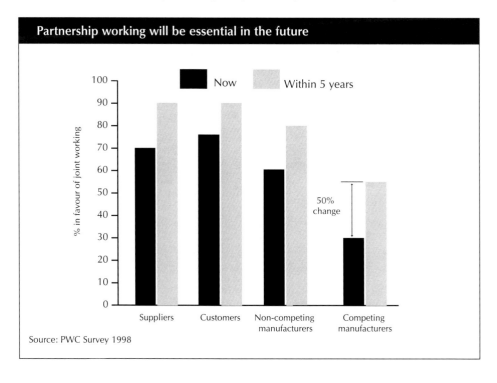

Partnership working will be essential in the future

Source: PWC Survey 1998

While there was little doubt about the advantages of co-venturing and partnerships with external organisations, real success stories were harder to come by. The reason for this is that partnerships are all too often seen as 'I win, you lose'. Often supply partners seek ways of reducing their own risk instead of creating genuine opportunities where both sides are winners.

Despite this gloomy picture, there was a general belief that the barriers to partnerships and co-venturing can be overcome and that there will be a significant shift towards real partnerships over the next five years.

These partnerships will include working with other non-competing manufacturers (favoured by 80%), competing manufacturers (55%), customers (90%), and suppliers (90%).

The survey also showed a clear and increasing tendency to focus on core business processes (in particular, brand and customer management, and new product introduction) and to outsource those activities seen as non-core (especially distribution and transport, and warehousing).

Imperative 5: integrating and synchronising the supply chain network

Survey participants believed that, within five years, 95% of supply chains will be demand-driven. The pace of change will depend on the business capability to meet three challenges:
- Building agility to meet changing market needs.
- Making market demand information readily available.
- Establishing robust relationships with customers and suppliers.

The key obstacles facing today's businesses as they strive to meet these challenges are:
- The sharing of demand information between customers and suppliers (this is often sensitive information and there is the threat of this being used as a competitive weapon against one of the partners).
- The integration of non-compatible IT systems.
- Manufacturing and supplier flexibility.
- Businesses must fully synchronise demand with supply and work tirelessly to fully integrate the external supply chain with their own.

Imperative 6: operations beyond the productivity edge

The demand-driven world shows a clear need to move to process management, but the necessity for operations excellence will not go away. Indeed, it will become more intense. However, the emphasis is likely to change:
- More manufacturing activities will be carried out downstream and closer to the customer, to allow differentiation as late as possible in the supply chain.
- There will be a renewed focus on manufacturing flexibility and reliability, to ensure agility.
- Global commodity-based sourcing will be increased.
- There will be a shift of administrative activities away from operations into shared service centres, to reduce costs as companies merge.
- Manufacturing will be measured against a new basket of performance measures (such as adherence to schedule and percentage of customer orders fulfilled, rather than on plant efficiency and quantity of product made).

Heavy investments in relationship management and supplier partnerships are prerequisites to obtain the operations excellence within process management. Furthermore, world class productivity must become a given.

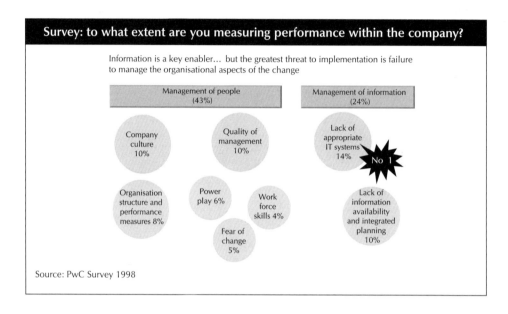

KEY ENABLERS

Imperative 7: business structure and organisation

What type of organisation — functional or process — is needed to face the challenges of globalisation? The response in the survey is overwhelming, with almost 80% indicating that their businesses will be driven by process management within the next five years. There was also a clear trend away from country-based structures towards multi-country product responsibilities.

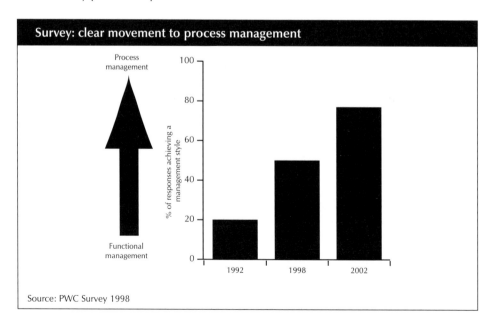

Imperative 8: process and performance measures

Performance measures are essential to understand supply chain performance and an important driver for improvement. The survey showed a lag in developing performance measures for a process-based versus a functional management approach — even though process management is seen as becoming the norm.

Furthermore, although most businesses have at least some performance measures in place, these are not comprehensive and significant gaps exist. In the future, leading edge practice must incorporate end-to-end supply chain performance measures to identify opportunities and to emphasise the importance of cross-functional management.

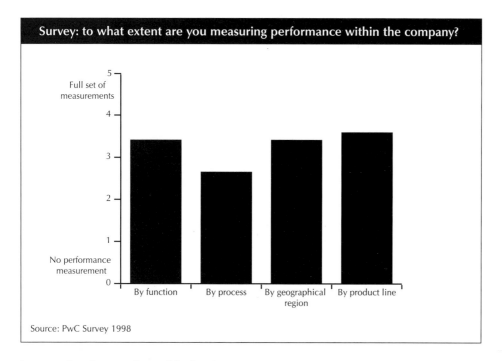

Survey: to what extent are you measuring performance within the company?

Source: PwC Survey 1998

Imperative 9: people and behaviours

No matter how appropriate the organisational structure and performance measures, change will happen only if individuals are willing and able to respond to the needs of market place and of the business.

A number of key changes are necessary in the mindset of managers and workforce alike to succeed in the supply chain age:

- A total commitment to customer service, governing everyday actions.
- An end-to-end supply chain mentality, influencing the way operational decisions are made.
- The pro-active management of customer demand, anticipating rather than following customer needs.
- A focus on the performance and success of the extended enterprise, from raw material suppliers to distributors or retailers.
- A switch from "stock push" to "demand pull" philosophy throughout the supply chain.
- The management of partnerships — no business can succeed on its own.

DO YOU REALIZE THAT SOMEONE IN YOUR COMPANY JUST ORDERED A $150 PENCIL?

This happens all the time, thanks to old-fashioned purchasing procedures. PeopleSoft eProcurement software automates your entire purchasing process so your employees can order their own office supplies from their desktops. Because PeopleSoft eProcurement is integrated with your ERP system, all purchases are automatically recorded in your financial and distribution systems, which helps control purchasing costs. Plus, it saves everybody time by steering employees toward approved items and suppliers via the Commerce One MarketSite.net™ business-to-business portal. Put an end to the old way of purchasing - visit our website or call for more information.

Introducing PeopleSoft eProcurement
Internet purchasing applications for the desktop

Buy Online • Utilizes Commerce One MarketSite.net™
Cuts Purchasing Costs • Integrates with ERP System

The survey revealed that managers and workforce do not possess the skills at present. Even worse, more than half of the businesses felt they were under-investing in the key areas required — operational best practice capability, organisational effectiveness skills, systems capability, change management capability, business process re-engineering skills, supply chain management capability and cost reduction skills. It is essential that these investments are made to stay competitive — indeed, to stay alive!

Imperative 10: high performance partnerships

Attitudes towards partnership are changing. The old-fashioned transactional relationships, based on a single point interface between two organisations, are totally inadequate to support the needs of the future supply chain.

Mutual dependency for business success on an effective end-to-end supply chain will encourage the development of true partnerships, with mutual investment, reward and risk for all parties. The growth in outsourcing and the increasing focus on core competence will continue to fuel the need.

The survey results show that the partnerships of today consist primarily of information sharing, but that within five years this will be superseded by partnerships that will represent joint management of the supply chain. A key requirement for future success is the ability to manage and leverage these partnerships.

Imperative 11: leveraging information and technology

A major paradox emerges from the survey regarding information and technology. It was overwhelmingly believed (80%) that IT can play a major role in optimising the supply chain. Yet the greatest single barrier to supply chain integration is the lack of appropriate IT systems. Current systems are simply not perceived as being fit for the purpose when it comes to supply chain integration and information visibility.

Most companies believe that the keys to solving the IT paradox are the completion of enterprise wide systems, and information transfer between supply chain players through e-commerce capability. The future drivers of benefit are beyond the enterprise resource planning (ERP) systems currently being implemented in a majority of the businesses.

The survey identified the following IT elements as the most important.

Foundation stones
- Reliable and efficient transaction data processing
- Provision of timely and accurate internationally visible information

Drivers of benefit
- Decision support information and advanced planning and scheduling (APS)
- Customer and supplier integration applications
- Electronic commerce

The last area, e-commerce, has enormous potential, as it allows customers and suppliers to shatter the barrier of incompatible IT systems. It will facilitate the exchange of information (for example, regarding stock levels, point of sale information, purchasing and delivery schedules and changes of orders) on an almost real-time basis.

MANAGING AT THE PACE OF CHANGE

Imperative 12: agility and ability to respond to change

The world is changing fast — faster perhaps than many businesses would wish. Excellence in supply chain management requires more than following the principles of best practice. The business must be able to respond quickly to particular customer needs and the changing business environment.

Agility is important at all levels of the business, from operational issues to strategic decisions. At the operational level, there is a need for flexibility and responsiveness to local and short-term variations in customer requirements. At the strategic level, agility is even more important, with the need to future-proof the business.

Respondents in the survey regarded board-level leadership as a critical ingredient for success. Not only to develop a supply chain vision, but also to continually refine business strategic direction and to drive implementation. The agility to respond to changing market circumstances is key to survival, and is, indeed, a competitive weapon in its own right.

Strategic change needs to be built into all tasks and not just revisited every year or so — the world is changing too quickly for this. The old model of strategy, design and implementation is dead. The future model will be vision-led, with continuous implementation, continuous benefits, and "proving by doing".

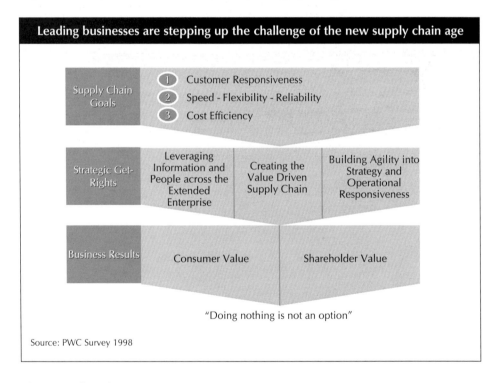

Leading businesses are stepping up the challenge of the new supply chain age

Supply Chain Goals	① Customer Responsiveness ② Speed - Flexibility - Reliability ③ Cost Efficiency		
Strategic Get-Rights	Leveraging Information and People across the Extended Enterprise	Creating the Value Driven Supply Chain	Building Agility into Strategy and Operational Responsiveness
Business Results	Consumer Value		Shareholder Value

"Doing nothing is not an option"

Source: PWC Survey 1998

The way ahead

The future of supply chains is both exciting and dynamic. The emerging global market will offer an unprecedented medium for growth, and those companies capable of harnessing e-commerce and emerging supply chain technologies will consistently surpass stakeholders' expectations.

Companies will form intimate relationships with their ever more demanding consumers. As a consequence, consumers will be delighted with the products and services they receive. After all, why shouldn't they? Everything will be invisibly tailored to fit their needs, using databases to suck data from a living and evolving interface with the consumer. Successful companies will long since have abandoned "pushing" to the market. Instead, they will sense and respond.

Data will become an undercurrent moving seamlessly between the end-to-end supply chain units. It will flow freely from the customer to business partners and create a knowledge-led organisation.

All business decisions will be made in real time, based on data shipped out of a data warehouse — the repository of all their internal and external information.

The supply chain will adjust continuously to achieve absolute customer satisfaction. Traditional supply chain assets will become limiting and will disappear in favour of flexible capabilities that can support a network organisation.

If traditional supply chain activities, such as logistics and finance, can be done better outside the organisation, they will be.

Additional expertise will be bought as required, but the learning organisation will seek to assimilate this expertise and minimise further demand as time goes by. True partnerships sharing risks and gains will be formed — even with competitors.

KEY ISSUES FOR THE CEO

- What role does the supply chain play in your organisation?
- How do you use it to maximise competitive advantage?
- What supply chain processes are core to your organisation?
- What are the key supply chain trends that are likely to impact your company?
- How are you addressing the 12 key imperatives for outstanding supply chain performance?
- What is it that your customers want from you, and how are you responding?
- How will your supply chain strategy help you cope with the changing business environment?

QUESTIONS ABOUT YOUR SUPPLY CHAIN?
WE HAVE THE ANSWERS.

What are we buying? Who are we buying from? How much are we spending with this supplier? What are we actually buying from that one? Reliable answers to such questions allow you to make purchasing decisions that result in huge savings. To achieve this you need access to timely, accurate information concerning every aspect of your supply chain.

The SAS® Solution for Supplier Relationship Management (SRM) enables you to understand all aspects of how, where what and why you buy, which in turn provides knowledge for smarter, more successful decision making.

Developed jointly by **SAS Institute,** the world leader in decision support software, and **Dun and Bradstreet,** the world's leading provider of business-to-business information, SRM consolidates and standardizes purchasing intelligence using Dun & Bradstreet's D-U-N-S numbers and UN/SPSC codes.

For more information on how to turn your supply chain questions into profitable answers, contact Chris Kelly at **ckelly@eur.sas.com** or visit us at **www.sas.com/app/srm.html**

The business of better decision making

SAS Institute

The consumer-centric supply chain

INTRODUCTION

A worldwide revolution has begun. A revolution that will radically alter the way we buy, sell and share goods, services and knowledge. This is the consumer-driven revolution.

This chapter focuses on the consumer and the various channels opening up for anticipating and capturing consumer demand. It addresses the challenges and opportunities facing retailers and suppliers of goods and services as they grapple with the issues that are emerging.

BACKGROUND

The 1980s and most of the 1990s were all about supplying customers and consumers at the lowest cost — the key word being supplying. From the manufacturer's perspective, this meant making and delivering in bulk quantities, thereby maximising operating efficiencies and reducing the cost of production.

Naturally, retailers only wanted what they could sell. This created a friction between retailers and suppliers over the trade-offs between bulk discounts, inventory ownership, frequency of delivery and other related issues that affected economies of scale.

Add to this the fact that retailers jealously guarded consumer data — and have been reluctant to share this with their suppliers — and the birth of supply chain management was inevitable.

In essence, supply chain management has been about coping with the problem while minimising the pain — dealing with the symptoms rather than the causes. As we move into the next millennium, the way we trade is switching from a focus on supply to a focus on demand — consumer demand.

In contrast to the characteristics of supply chain management, demand-led flows are all about consumer service, mass customisation, time to market and, above all, the cost of service as opposed to the cost of production.

It is difficult to avoid the conclusion that, in a saturated market, retailers and consumer packaged goods (CPG) companies are working harder and harder for less and less reward.

Working harder and harder for less and less

Consider the following picture of intense competition.

- The average US consumer receives 1 million marketing messages per year — roughly 3,000 per day — at a cost of $300 billion a year in 1996.
- The number of new product launches in the US will increase by 10%–16% by 2001.
- US food manufacturers spent $25 billion on promotions in 1996 — about twice the profit margin of the US food retailing industry. For the consumer packaged goods sector as a whole, trade promotion spending totals $70 billion annually, or up to 15% of revenues.

Now consider the results.

- Since 1991 retail sales per square foot in the US have declined by 17.3% in real terms, despite initiatives such as the efficient consumer response.
- Visits to supermarkets are down from 2.2 times a week to 1.8.
- The average US store contains 40,000 grocery items. The average consumer tends to be interested in about 150.
- Non-auto retail spending in the US has fallen from 45% of total consumer spending in 1970 to 35% in 1997. The only CPG items to show growth in the US in 1997 were candy/gum and snacks — at 2%.
- CPG sales have decreased across Europe since 1990, by rates that range from -0.4% in Finland to -6.6% in Greece. In Japan, food and clothing expenditure as a proportion of total consumer spending is declining year on year.
- A survey of over 24,000 recent new product launches in Europe found that 86% had less than 50% distribution after one year. It also found that only 540 items could be classified as totally new.

Not only is the market saturated, but retailers are responding in a number of ways that are potentially detrimental to CPG companies' interests.

- They are squeezing margins as they seek to compete on price.
- They are stretching their brands into new areas — financial services, utilities, Internet service provision and so on — which will further strengthen the brand franchise that they have relative to individual CPG brands.
- Especially in Europe, they are seeking to build their own brand strength — for example, own brand sales rose by 28% in Europe between 1993 and 1998, and one European chain has recently elected to go wholly own-brand.

Something has to give. The evidence suggests a business model that is serving companies less and less well. Fundamentally, there are too many products, and perhaps, too many companies are chasing too few consumers. This means that businesses have to run faster and faster just to stand still.

As companies seek to respond there are a number of trends that they should consider. These trends have been in evidence for a while, but when they are extrapolated into the future they change the picture dramatically.

The current business model is failing, and the rules of the game are changing.

REVOLUTION OR E-VOLUTION?

In Marxist theory, revolution is defined as the violent and historically necessary transition from one system of production in a society to the next, as from feudalism to capitalism.

All revolutions need a catalyst. Political revolutions, such as the overthrow of a government, often start with the assassination of a significant figure of state. The consumer-driven revolution started far less dramatically with the advent of the Internet.

The Internet has effectively opened up Pandora's box for all to see. The technology has enabled consumers to have a real say in terms of their individual needs and for this information to be captured in real time by manufacturers and retailers in ways only dreamt of previously.

However, the information channel enabled by the Internet is wider than just the exchange between the consumer and the supplier or retailer of goods and services. It is also about the ability to exploit business-to-business opportunities. Regardless of the channel, retailer-to-consumer, manufacturer-to-consumer, business-to-business or pure Internet trading, one common thread exists throughout — the consumer.

Competitive edge will come only from having a clear understanding of consumers' needs and organising everything a retailer or supplier does around them — in effect, putting the consumer at the heart of strategy, people and processes.

CONSUMER-CENTRICITY

The consumer-driven revolution is about being consumer-centric. Consumer-centricity is about maintaining competitive advantage through building deep consumer knowledge, not just consumer data or even information.

For example, manufacturers have argued long and hard for retailers to provide them with their customers' EPOS/loyalty card data. The big question is what would they be able to do with several terabytes of raw data coming down the network daily? The answer is probably not a lot!

It is about deploying this knowledge not just as a consumer focus, but right into an organisation's corporate DNA. In this way, it becomes possible to create and maintain a continuous fit between the creation and provision of products and services and the evolving consumer needs.

THREE BIG CHALLENGES

Becoming a consumer-centric business relies on three things.
Relating to consumers — as equal parties in permanent relationships, that won't just consume what they are given — and managing the relationship as the key competitive asset.

Exploiting technologies — such as e-commerce, consumer database management and digital TV, to deepen understanding and deliver value in new ways to even smaller segments — possibly at the level of the individual.

Reworking — every aspect of the business value chain back from the consumer, including offer, processes, systems, structure, skills and physical assets — to support the relationship with each segment or individual.

The business emphasis needs to shift from the provision of products or services to solutions, and from transaction management to relationship management.

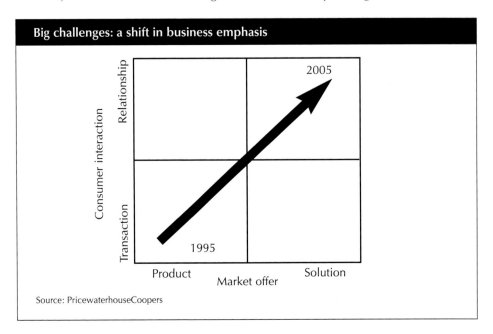

Big challenges: a shift in business emphasis

Source: PricewaterhouseCoopers

The challenge of relating to consumers

Consumers are experiencing nothing short of a revolution in the range of new channels available to them to choose and buy goods and services. The revolution is being driven by emerging technologies such as the Internet, mobile phones, DVD multimedia and digital TV. These technologies represent both an opportunity and a threat to traditional retail and supply chain operations.

Through these new channels, information about goods and services is becoming increasingly easy and cheap to come by and is almost ubiquitous in its nature. Consumers are becoming used to having information at their fingertips. They no longer have to rely on walking from store to store to collate and compare offers and prices. They simply have to sit in front of an Internet-enabled computer and browse the market wherever and whenever they wish. Furthermore, the attraction of multimedia and increased service levels is enhancing the experience on the Web, and people are starting to enjoy using it.

As a result of the richness of information available to them, consumers are becoming more knowledgeable of the market place and more discerning over where and what they buy. As a result, consumer values and preferences are evolving rapidly, presenting a challenge to companies to keep up with consumers' changing tastes and values.

The rate of growth of the emerging channels is further accelerated by the low cost of entry. New entrants can appear quickly and cheaply. Existing players will have to react fast before new entrants establish a brand presence and trust with the rapidly growing, Internet-aware consumer population. It is eminently possible for new entrants to traditional markets to oust well established players through lower cost bases.

In reaction, some extraordinary measures are being taken by traditional retailers. Recently, in San Francisco for example, Kinder Toys moved from its physical shops to virtual ones leaving the message in its shop windows: 'We have moved to www.toydomain.com'.

The same technologies that are causing consumer behaviour to change rapidly also make it easier to track those changes and be more in touch with the consumer. It is through the innovative use of these technologies that companies will be able to forge stronger relationships with their consumer base.

Companies are learning that it is good to be ever more hungry for information about their customers. They understand the value of deriving, from historical information, real knowledge about their customers to build individual profiles about each of them. In doing so, they acknowledge the presence of so-called "markets of one" as opposed to the "one market of many". They embellish the knowledge with innovative thinking to try to anticipate their customers' future needs. They look to adapt their product and service offerings to preserve or improve their performance and success in the future.

It is clear that to preserve and grow their relationships with the consumers, businesses need to use a vehicle that has not been traditionally used in the past — technology.

The challenge of technology

Emerging communications and computing technology are transforming our lives and the way we do business. However, the challenge has always been to fully appreciate the potential of new technology, as history shows. The trick is clearly to be creative and innovative, but with foresight. To do this successfully, organisations must extend their normal boundaries of thinking.

Technology forecasting: getting it wrong

"I think there is a world market for maybe five computers."

Thomas Watson, chairman of IBM, 1943

"There is no reason anyone would want a computer in their home."

Kenlsen, president, chairman and founder, Digital Equipment Corp, 1977

"This 'telephone' has too many short-comings to be seriously considered as a means of communication."

Western Union internal memo, 1876

There is a plethora of new technologies that are changing the way organisations connect to each other and to the consumer. These technologies enable connectivity, just as supply chain management does — connectivity between value chains across different businesses in different industries. And, most importantly, this connectivity includes the end-user — the consumer.

These technologies include the development of distributed application development tools such as Java and CORBA, which allow the applications on different computers to talk to each other and automatically run processes dynamically and interactively on each other's platforms.

There is the new U-TMS mobile phone technology, due out in 2001, that will support fast Internet access. Within three years, the Teledesic satellite system will provide the Internet in the sky with 2000 times the current performance of typical modem access.

Tricks of technology — from microwave to bank

NCR, normally associated with cash-point machines and EPOS terminals, recently developed a microwave bank to demonstrate how easy it is to turn the concept of Internet access in the home into both a banking terminal and a mini supply chain management tool.

Essentially a microwave oven, with a touch sensitive colour screen on the door, it allows people to browse the Internet from the kitchen, or watch television without taking up any additional space.

It is also a bank because it securely facilitates purchases and financial transactions and directly links to the consumer's bank account.

In addition, it is a supply chain management tool for the home, since it also includes a barcode reader. The idea is that goods are scanned in as cupboards are stocked up after shopping, and used cartons and tins are scanned out as they are thrown away. A running inventory is thereby kept.

This presents the possibility of a fully integrated supply chain management relationship between the household and the retailer.

These technologies continue to evolve rapidly and converge, with innovative combinations of new technology beginning to emerge.

Specific packages are now available to help companies in their management of relationships with customers. Generically known as customer relationship management (CRM) systems, they allow customer profiles and information to be stored to support interactions with the customer. For example, call centres will use such systems to automatically display relevant customer data when the customer calls. Such information might include records of any recent complaints, outstanding orders, and new products recently ordered.

While CRM systems tend to be installed within, and maintained by, an individual company, new technology is providing the means of acquiring and maintaining this data from external sources — the new connective channels to market.

Consumers access the Internet through an Internet Service Provider (ISP). There are many ISPs offering their services. Some are offshoots from traditional telecommunication companies, such as British Telecom's Lineone. Others have grown up with the Internet (such as UUNet and AmericaOnline). Some are new entrants leveraging their customer base, such as the Freeserve product from the UK electrical retailer, Dixon's. When an individual logs on to the Internet, they are invariably taken to the home page of the ISP. From there, they are offered additional services, such as free e-mail facilities, newsgroups and chat rooms.

ISPs offer consumers their window on the Web — an anchor point that brings a sense of order to the Internet world. This view of the Internet, delivered to the consumer by the ISP, is often referred to as a portal. However, it is not only ISPs that offer portals. For example, search engines such as Yahoo and Altavista are portals. The famous virtual bookseller Amazon.com is also a portal, as is Barclays Bank.

Portal administrators are in a unique position to monitor individuals as they surf the Internet. It is possible, for example, to collate information about what types of Web sites are visited, what kind of activities are performed, and how much time is spent on the Web. Collating that information allows a profile to be built up quickly about an individual — the knowledge of what kind of person they are and what they like doing.

In learning about individual consumers, the ISP can start to tailor its services for them specifically. For example, if a particular person accesses stock market sites regularly, the ISP might start sending them headlines of financial news as and when it breaks. This directing — or pushing — of information towards individuals to meet their specific requirements is sometimes referred to as push technology.

It is clear that the consumer must feel comfortable with the profiling concept. This will take time to settle, and acceptance of profiling will emerge slowly but surely, possibly along the following lines:

The first year
- ISPs/portals create profiles for each individual.
- Companies buy access to profiles, with the consumer's permission, and create and offer new services and products to individuals.
- Consumers initially like the tailored products and services they are offered, and learn the benefits of having their profile known by trusted companies.

The second year
- After an initial honeymoon period, some companies start to abuse the profiles and the junk offer emerges.
- People become more discerning about who they offer their profile to.
- Independent arbiters emerge who act on behalf of the consumer to filter out offers that do not match their profile.

The third year
- Some arbiters miss the mark. Their filtering is too weak in some cases and too strong in others (in the latter case the consumer is denied key opportunities). So individuals seek a better profile arbiter.
- A new market of profile arbiters emerges.
- Profiles and profile arbiters become a way of life.

Owning the rights to access knowledge contained in individual profiles to predict what preferences the customer might have is clearly compelling to businesses. Some companies have been quick to notice this and even those not traditionally associated with the Internet have acted early to capture the profiling opportunity, as in the case of Barclays Bank.

A reasonable objective for these new portals might be to achieve a critical mass of profiled users in as short a time as possible. The means of achieving this is often the offer of free access to the Internet and, more recently, free provision of computers to browse the Internet.

So companies have the choice of becoming, or buying into, portals or profile arbiters, or in ensuring that they have the means of securing the data they need and storing it on their own consumer databases. The most successful companies will arguably be those that use this database and customer relationship management technology to interpret the data from every possible angle and understand and respond to their customer base better.

One question that will dominate thinking in the next few years is who will become the profile arbiters of tomorrow? Will it be, for example, a network of banks or an alliance of manufacturers? ISPs, portals and mobile phone networks are also possible profile arbiters. Or will it be a totally new entrant?

When speculating about the future of consumer behaviour, it is generally accepted that the shopping experience will never be totally replaced by the Internet. People enjoy looking around and trying things before they buy, particularly in the welcoming ambience of modern shopping malls. And nothing will replace the smell of freshly baked bread!

In accordance with Moore's Law —that the pace of change is such that the amount of data that can be stored on a microchip doubles every 18 to 24 months — technology and communications continue to get faster, smaller and cheaper. With the advent of global satellite networks by circa 2002, Internet access will be available anywhere in the world, from the heart of the Sahara desert to aircraft flying over the middle of the Pacific Ocean.

It will not be long before high-performance, pocket sized personal communicators will emerge which have a built-in mobile phone, high resolution screen and real-time Internet access. It will also be securely loaded with electronic money. It is perhaps worth painting a scenario of the future to imagine what such technology might bring in a few years' time.

Latest technology meets the shopping mall

A person walks in to a shopping mall and has their profile automatically communicated to the mall's own profile arbiter. In return, they receive a multimedia map of the mall showing the location of all the shops.

A dialogue continues between the personal communicator and the profile arbiter for a few seconds. The individual is then buzzed with a short tune that signifies that there are some special offers that may interest them since they last visited the mall. The person takes a look on the screen. There may be 50 of these, of which they acknowledge 10 and perhaps browse more information on three.

The 10 that are selected are fed back to the relevant retail outlets in the mall. The person's route around the mall is planned for them on the screen. It takes account of the fact that they like a tea break after about an hour, and plans that in for them at the Olde Tea Shoppe in the middle of the mall. Meanwhile, the retail outlets expect their visit.

Clearly the person may deviate away from plan if something grabs their attention in a particular shop. When they do so, their profile is updated. All products and services in which they show an interest are automatically registered through their personal communicator to the profile arbiter, and their profile is updated.

The profile arbiter service will offer consumers additional value-added information. For example, it will monitor sales of all products and services to an individual. Acting as the consumer's virtual friend, it tells them about their changing preferences and asks them if they agree with those changes.

It also takes a note of the products they have shown an interest in, but haven't yet bought — perhaps a kitchen unit or a watch. It makes a judgement on how serious their interest was based on how much time they spent on it, or how many they've looked at recently.

It then offers the manufacturers and retailers information on the products that the person has shown an interest in at a nominal fee. It may even offer it to the manufacturer's suppliers.

In return, they will get to know much more about their end customer's behaviour, since they are getting the information directly sourced from the consumer and not the retailer. Their costs of serving the consumer go down — as do their marketing expenses, time and development costs of new products and services.

The profile arbiter effectively becomes the connector between the different nodes of the supply chain for all the products that an individual buys or shows an interest in. Across a population of many individuals, the value of this information becomes significant.

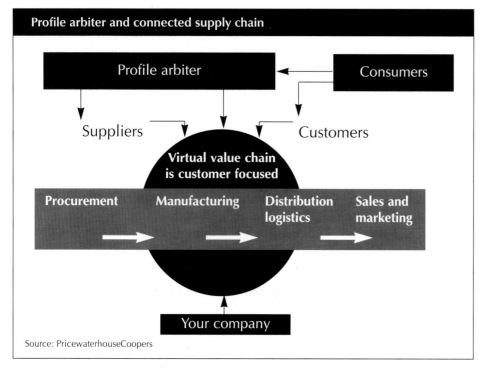

Profile arbiter and connected supply chain

Source: PricewaterhouseCoopers

The profile arbiters undertake to act fairly on behalf of both the supplier and the consumer. It will collate and analyse information, deriving new trends and alerting supply chain subscribers.

The concept of extending technology to shopping can extend beyond the home and the mall. Even when people are mobile, perhaps out in their car, the combination of mobile phone and satellite web technology will come into its own.

For example, if an individual registers on their profile that they are in leisure mode then the screen in their car might list all the leisure sites and services that may be of interest to them within, say, 30 miles. If they are travelling on business, their travel details will have been entered automatically into their profile. On their way to the airport, they are warned of traffic problems and flight delays.

New information — say linking business travellers' locations with weather patterns and soft drink or ice cream buying — could create new markets via these screens in cars.

As companies embark on e-business to improve service, reduce costs and open new channels, competitive landscapes within and across industries will become transformed. The rapid pace of advancement means it is becoming more and more difficult to keep up.

A dilemma facing many business managers is whether to be proactive or reactive — to lead or be led. Each option has its own risks and opportunities. Lead too early and you stumble across problems you never anticipated because you did not have the benefit of experience to draw from. Act too late and you'll be left behind as others take advantage of being first in the market.

What is clear is that a new generation of consumers is fast emerging and all companies need to respond — particularly among the younger generation who are growing up with the Internet and emerging technologies.

THE CHALLENGE OF REWORKING

Clearly, many opportunities and uncertainties exist as the new channels to market and underlying technology drivers evolve. Companies must use the new insights to review their customer base and, perhaps, split off parts of it to distributors in order to reduce cost.

Segmentation of the retained customer base would enable different service levels to be offered to strategic, core and standard customers, reducing the cost of serving them but at the same time meeting all of the retained customers' requirements.

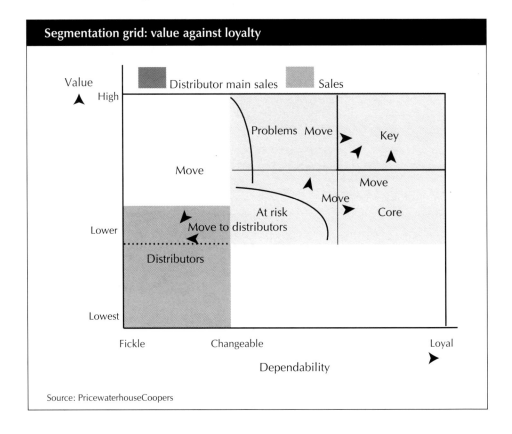

Segmentation grid: value against loyalty

Source: PricewaterhouseCoopers

Those split off to distributors could still be supported by a virtual brand conveyed to the distributor through extranet technology (extending a company's intranet to privileged third parties).

To survive against the decreasing barriers of entry to markets, it is clear that companies will have to revert to their core strengths to maximise their resilience. Anything that is not core must have the cost ripped out of it, perhaps through outsourcing to a tightly connected partner.

Knowledge management must be used to ensure that the valuable knowledge companies acquire about the consumers is shared across the organisation and is always available when and where it is needed.

The challenge is to employ the same technologies that permit connectivity between organisations within the organisation. Innovative architectures employing portals and push technology will be applied by the companies that excel in this respect.

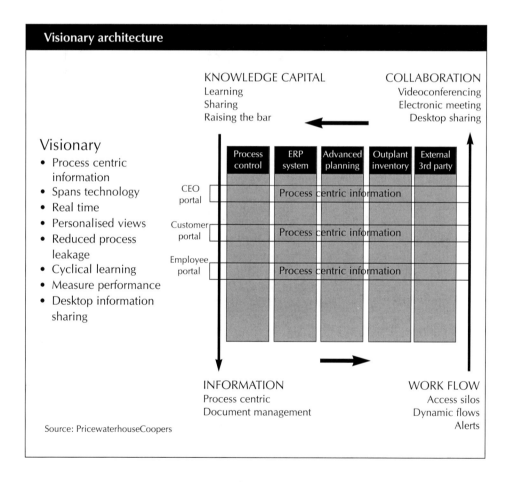

Visionary architecture

Source: PricewaterhouseCoopers

Innovative and tightly connected partnerships, both horizontally and vertically, with the best performers in the supply and demand chains, will need to be formed to offer new complete packages and service offers.

In understanding customers' true behaviour and requirements, one might need to re-visit completely your customer base. New metrics for measuring the value of customers may be needed — for example, using lifetime value instead of year-on-year margin. Using new appropriate metrics will permit new ways to categorise the customer base.

All businesses are being presented with new challenges at an ever increasing rate of change. Perhaps only the most agile, foresighted and broad minded will survive.

KEY ISSUES FOR THE CEO

- How will your business respond to a world full of profile arbiters?
- How will you get access to the behavioural information being offered by the profile arbiter and tailor your product development and marketing programme accordingly?
- How will you ensure a strong brand presence on the Web?
- Who will you partner to do all the things you need to achieve?
- What does your organisation have that would be very difficult for a new entrant to emulate?
- What is stopping someone else from doing exactly what you do without all the legacy systems, processes and organisation that you have?

Selling in cyberspace — the brave new world of retailing

INTRODUCTION

This chapter looks at the current state of electronic retailing — e-tailing — and where it might go from here. It discusses the critical factors for a successful e-tailing operation and their implications for the physical delivery of the product. It also defines the new business models that will change the retail sector for ever.

This chapter shows that the new technology is changing the rules for retailers. Although not all traditional retailing businesses will be swept away, there are new threats and new opportunities. Any strategy to compete is likely to require a substantial change in many of the current processes. Customer relationships are transformed, distribution and logistics may be more complex, brand management is extended to new channels, and information systems to support these processes will be required. The overall trends are clear.

- Co-everything — alliances and partnerships are replacing linear supply chains and integrated enterprises. Outsourcing is becoming commonplace, as critical new skills are required at increasing pace.
- Technology — consumers, as well as businesses, are getting more connected.
- Intangible value — companies are valued for customer relationships and knowledge, and brands rather than physical assets.
- Service offerings are overtaking products — customers want information, customisation and advice, not just products.

E-TAILING

Nobody, as yet, appears to be making money selling on the Internet. Certainly, organisations making profits from e-tailing are hard to find. In most cases, the basic economics of fulfilment — satisfying customer requirements in a profitable manner — are far from clear. Generally, customers want wider product ranges, more convenient ordering, customised products, home delivery — and all for less money.

But a brief look at statistics shows that the impact of e-tailing has been variable, it has yet to affect many sectors in a big way. For the purchase of computers, one of the leading sectors, forecasts show 16% of transactions being online by 2003. Some of the largest retail sectors are likely to be little affected. Clothing and groceries are predicted to have under 1% of sales by then.

Case study: eToys, Dixons' Freeserve

Two examples highlight the difficulties of finding the right valuation of these new e-tailers.

eToys is a two-year-old toy e-tailer operating in the US market. It went public on May 20, 1999, tripling its value on the first day of trading to $7.78 billion. This represented a premium of 38% on Toys R Us, the traditional store-based market leader.

But compare the two firms' turnover. eToys' revenues in 1998 were $30 million (on which it lost $28.6 million). Toys R Us achieved sales of $11.2 billion in the same year.

A similar picture of wild demand for an Internet stock occurred in the UK after Dixons, a retailer of consumer electronics and communication equipment, launched its free access Internet service, Freeserve. The service is a hybrid of Internet business models, but over 90% of its revenues are expected to come from electronic retailing and advertising by 2003.

The success of this service in attracting customers — over 1.3m since launch in 1998 — tripled Dixons' share price between June 1998 and April 1999. In the summer of 1999, Freeserve's flotation — initially valued at £1.3 billion on revenues of just £2.7 million — was massively oversubscribed.

However, this is a critical time in terms of positioning. The total online retail market will be worth around £3.1 billion in the UK by 2003. Worldwide it could reach $100 billion that year. It is now clearly the time for senior management to assess how these changes will affect their organisation, and see what can be done to ensure that they come out on top.

As with all change, this revolution brings enormous opportunities and significant threats. New on-line entrants — the e-tailers — are taking market share from established, traditional players; manufacturers, such as Nike, Unilever and Levi's, are selling direct to consumers; and, established retailers are opening new demand and supply channels. There is frenzied activity in the boardrooms as strategies to prosper, or at least survive, are formulated.

Much of the predicted increase in Internet sales will be cannibalised from existing store and catalogue sales. With the huge fixed costs of running a traditional retail business, losing sales to a new channel can be disastrous — the effect of losing 5% of sales to an on-line competitor will typically reduce net profit by 20%.

The picture in the US, the most advanced on-line market, is of a bloodbath. There are price wars in all the leading sectors — the books/CD market is a prime example. In the fight for market share and access to customers, profits have become a secondary driver. It is very difficult to provide Internet shopping profitably.

So, for example, Peapod is a virtual, on-line supermarket operating in the US. It had a market capitalisation of $210 million in 1998. It has never made a profit, and has direct costs 13% higher than revenues.

Alternatively, Borders is the second largest traditional book retailer in the US, with 1,145 stores. It has felt obliged to react to the changes in the market caused by the rise of amazon.com and it opened a Web site in May 1998. It has now joined the on-line discount war and invested in a new distribution centre. Start up losses are mounting ($20 million in 1999), and the company's stock has fallen by about 40% as a reaction.

The supply chain challenge

Traditional retailing is characterised by having a substantial network of stores, displaying a range of products — in many cases, a very large range (25,000-50,000 and upwards for supermarkets and department stores).

The supply chain challenge has been to replenish the stores effectively — to achieve required product availability in store. This is usually achieved by holding another layer of product inventory in one or more warehouses, which are in turn replenished from product manufacturers or suppliers.

Store numbers and location have been viewed as a substantial asset, and a significant entry barrier to new entrants. In the UK grocery market, Tesco has over 600 stores, J Sainsbury over 500. US supermarket group Wal-Mart has over 3500 stores worldwide.

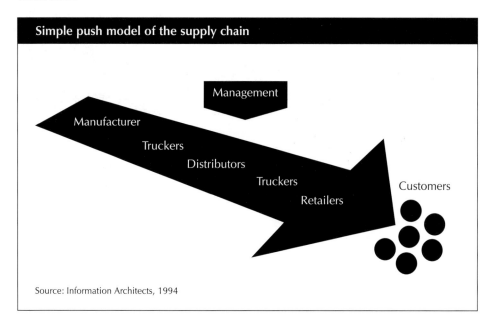

Simple push model of the supply chain

Management

Manufacturer

Truckers

Distributors

Truckers

Retailers

Customers

Source: Information Architects, 1994

Market share is gained through extending the store network — by acquiring new sites, or an existing chain. The process of acquiring sites, and then building or refurbishment, can be lengthy, and this has generally meant that change in the retail sector is gradual.

ON-LINE ACCESS CHANGES THE RULES

Among the emerging trends in retail have been consolidation and globalisation. Wal-Mart, the world's largest retailer, has grown by offering, among other things, a large range of products under one roof, taking market share from small local stores. Scale brings with it economies from buying, as well as operating costs.

On-line access provides the ultimate in consolidation — the Web is effectively one big town. Physical store locations fragment the market while on-line access has the power to create super-consolidation.

The cliché for retailing success has been "location, location, and location" — meaning physical location on the high street or the mall. But the example of amazon.com shows that these rules are changing — the most valuable book retailer has not a single store.

Now the word location is likely to have a different meaning — a place on the Web page of a leading service provider. Barnes and Noble is paying AOL $40 million to be its exclusive bookseller for four years.

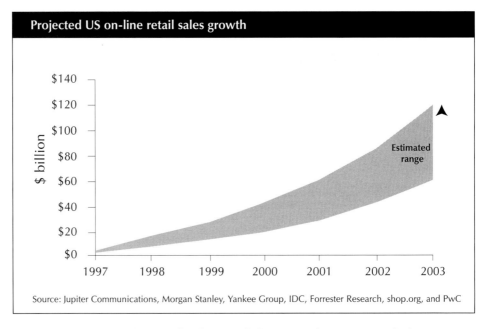

Projected US on-line retail sales growth

Source: Jupiter Communications, Morgan Stanley, Yankee Group, IDC, Forrester Research, shop.org, and PwC

The rise of Internet shopping has been well documented. Latest research shows 11.6 million regular Internet users in the UK — 25% of the country's adult population. Dixon's Freeserve alone has over a million customers, 40% of whom are first-time Internet users. From a low base — just 0.2% of all sales currently in the UK — growth is predicted to be explosive. Estimates range from 2.5% for all sales in the UK to 6% in the US by 2003.

The factors that have caused this are clear. Technology is, of course, the enabler — widespread access to the Internet, more rapid data exchange, and user-friendly browsers.

However, at the same time, there has been a constraint in the amount of family leisure time available. For example, a Harris poll in 1997 showed the median number of hours worked per week in the US rising from 40.6 in 1973 to 50.6 in 1995. The number of dual-earner households is also increasing.

Mundane tasks such as grocery shopping, banking and dry cleaning are using an increasing proportion of the shrinking time available. There is the attractive prospect

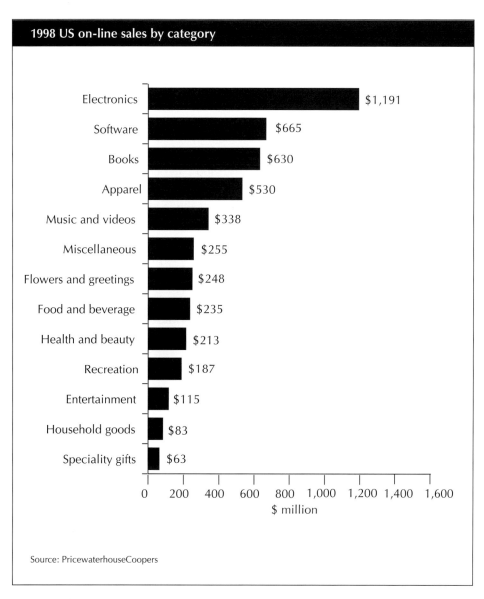

1998 US on-line sales by category

Category	$ million
Electronics	$1,191
Software	$665
Books	$630
Apparel	$530
Music and videos	$338
Miscellaneous	$255
Flowers and greetings	$248
Food and beverage	$235
Health and beauty	$213
Recreation	$187
Entertainment	$115
Household goods	$83
Speciality gifts	$63

$ million

Source: PricewaterhouseCoopers

of accomplishing some of these tasks by a few hours of Web surfing, accompanied by home delivery and automatic payment. One survey found that only 11% of Americans like grocery shopping — and 83% believe it takes too much time.

Consumers have also realised that choice has widened. Their Web browser has global access, and they can compare products and prices with minimum time and effort.

Clearly, some areas of retailing are more suited to Internet access than others. The chart here shows that the leading categories are similar to those that have been popular with mail-order shoppers — Internet ordering has increased this trend. The demographics of Internet shoppers is significant in its prospects — the average age of British users is 33.

The motives of on-line shoppers are still developing. In the UK, current usage is still dominated by the time-poor, affluent users which retailers love. Just 23% cited price as a main reason for on-line buying — against 57% citing convenience. In the US bargain hunting is much more prevalent — 80% put price in their top three considerations.

CRITICAL SUCCESS FACTORS IN E-TAILING

Setting up and running a successful e-retailing operation involves a numbers of factors.

Business proposition

The overall business proposition must be coherent, and must contain an attractive customer offering. Nobody would claim that on-line shopping offers everything to all. Bookshops with comfortable chairs and coffee shops, and market stalls with fresh produce one can see and smell, will surely have a part to play for a while yet.

The proposition for any new venture must be carefully judged. Specifically, a business proposition for electronic shopping must consider:
- What assortment of products to offer.
- What other services to offer.
- How to interact with the customer.
- How to manage the relationship with the customer — in the short and long term.
- How to market the business proposition.

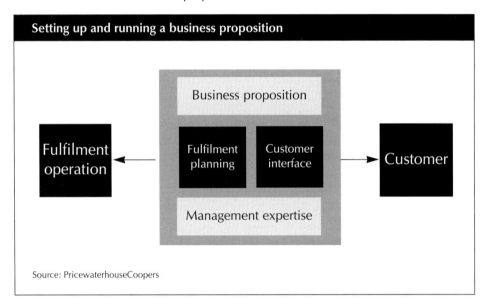

Setting up and running a business proposition

Source: PricewaterhouseCoopers

Wal-Mart has become the world's largest retailer by offering convenience, price and product breadth. It is unlikely that these simple keys to retailing success will change in the on-line world. In fact, there are opportunities to considerably extend these concepts. When considering the proposition to offer, it is useful to look at different customer requirements and how different channels, or companies, meet them.

Clearly, on-line selling will only prosper if it offers a better proposition overall to at least one sector of consumers. For this, a good understanding of different consumer types is crucial.

Customer interface

Customer access is, in many cases, a barrier to growth in on-line shopping. Setting up a Web-based selling organisation, and marketing the service, can be expensive.

Once attracted to the site, it is critical to convert lookers into buyers. Currently, many users do not buy for a number of reasons. There are concerns about security of payment systems, about speed of access and about the difficulty of navigating the Web site. Studies show that only 17% of Internet users buy within a year of getting online.

The future will see a move towards non-PC platforms as the leading form of access to the Internet. Digital television will increase the access to on-line services over the next five years. After this, other devices — Webphones, for example — will emerge to further fuel the growth.

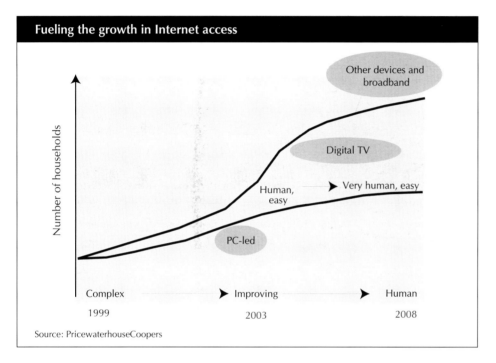

Fueling the growth in Internet access

Source: PricewaterhouseCoopers

The future of retailing will be through multiple channels to consumers. The choice of channel will depend on many factors — the product lines, the type of consumer, the consumer's geographical location. For example, staple items are best ordered remotely and delivered. For some consumers, the purchase of gifts and fresh food requires close-up attention, so a store visit is appropriate. On-line shopping then provides a further alternative channel to market for retailers.

Exploiting new channels, outsourcing

An organisation will require different skills and expertise to exploit these new channels to market. In many cases, these skills will be most easily and conveniently acquired through partnerships and alliances. Recruiting and training processes to establish in-house capability are often too slow and cumbersome to keep up with market requirements.

As the channels to market multiply, and complexity increases, it is impractical for a single company to master all areas. This is especially true in start-up phases of new ventures. No company wants to invest heavily to test demand where the outcome is uncertain. As business develops, it may be decided to bring more functions in-house.

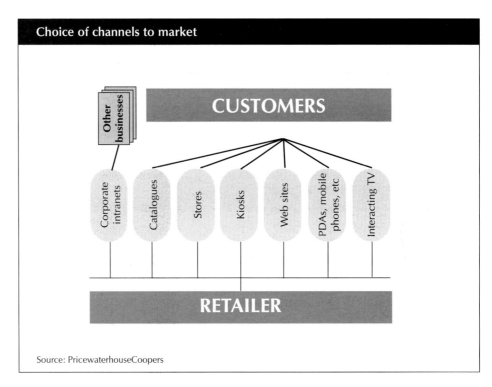

Choice of channels to market

CUSTOMERS

Other businesses

Corporate intranets
Catalogues
Stores
Kiosks
Web sites
PDAs, mobile phones, etc
Interacting TV

RETAILER

Source: PricewaterhouseCoopers

For example, Wal-Mart has outsourced its entire Internet shopping operation to Fingerhut Business Services. Fingerhut is a catalogue and online retail specialist and will handle order processing, warehousing, shipping and customer services. It is likely that an offering of up to 80,000 products will be available, with 48-hour delivery. This move is a big step forwards in this area for Wal-Mart, and has been achieved with minimal investment through outsourcing.

Fulfilment

Much has been made of the impacts of e-tailing on customer interfaces. The pricing of Internet companies is usually measured per customer rather than by sales or profits. In the current market conditions, a large customer base is seen as success: profits can wait until later.

Eventually, of course, all successful companies must be able to serve their customers profitably. Annual sales growth, leading edge technology and high numbers of Web-page hits may impress the markets in the short term, but do not guarantee profits.

In time, Internet retailing companies will be priced as retailers, not as technology companies. When the dust settles, the winners in the new world of retailing will have mastered the sales and marketing aspects of the new technology. But, critically, they must also be able to provide leading edge service in product delivery. They must be able to offer an attractive business proposition, and be able to fulfil it profitably.

The Internet has re-written the rules on how products are delivered. In many cases the retailers have taken over the extra burden of delivering to the customer's home. Products may be individually tailored to customer requirements, such as with Dell Computers. Some products can even be delivered in digital form down a telephone line, such as music, news, films, publications and information.

Teething problems and more

It is clear that there have been big early problems in companies providing poorly thought out, under-resourced, propositions.

- A Swiss watch company omitted to tell UK customers about hidden tax and handling costs incurred by online orders fulfilled from Switzerland.
- Christmas 1998 saw a large increase in Internet shopping — afterwards many companies had problems with inadequate returns procedures, as unwanted gifts were sent back or exchanged
- Supermarkets are being forced into loss-making home delivery services. One leading UK supermarket chain, for example, picks customer orders from store shelves, incurring all the store replenishment costs on top of the extra picking and delivery expenses.

Retailing is a low margin business. For example, Morgan Stanley research in 1997 showed only a 2.1% net margin average for a sample of US retailers. There is little room to incur extra cost and still make profits. The supply chain must not just respond to the changes, but must lead the charge to transform the market as customer requirements change. The rules of the game are changing — the winners of the corporate battle will be those who adapt most quickly and in the most effective way.

IMPLICATIONS FOR DELIVERING THE PRODUCT

There are enormous difficulties in making a profit from on-line retailing. The challenges for companies in delivering products are in many cases as significant as those for communicating with them. Retailers, or suppliers, will often need major resources and expertise to provide:

- Individually customised products.
- Sources of a wide product range.
- On-line information on order progress.
- Picking and packing in very small quantities.
- Home delivery — again in small loads.
- Management of returns.

A good example of the challenge is in the difficult area of grocery retailing. It is a huge market, with a spend of over £90 billion in the UK alone, and uses a lot of consumer time. It is difficult to establish on-line selling because of a number of factors:

- Large product ranges are typical, causing difficulties in maintaining catalogues and in ordering.
- Fresh, chilled and frozen foods require special handling, and cannot be left on doorsteps for any length of time.
- Generally goods are bulky, and hence expensive to handle and deliver.
    However, an effective customer service proposition could tap into a huge potential market if it incorporates:
- Easy Internet ordering.
- Economical and effective home delivery.
- Good product availability and freshness.

Current grocery firms are burdened with huge chains of stores and their replenishment systems are not easily adapted to home delivery. Margins in the UK are wider than many other countries, but still only around 6% is typical.

There are a number of stand-alone catalogue and Internet players, and the established chains have reacted by setting up their own services.

In the US, Peapod and Scotty's have established themselves in certain regions. In the UK Tesco, Sainsbury and Asda have the largest presence. Iceland is well established in the frozen food sector.

Most of these services make an extra charge (between £2 and £5 for the UK companies), and customers tend to be households that are short of time and are happy to pay extra.

No great profits are being made. Different fulfilment models have been followed to enter the market — for example, Tesco is picking customer deliveries from its larger stores, while Sainsbury and other chains are setting up dedicated picking centres as current supermarket warehouses are not suited to picking small individual orders.

The following chart shows how these approaches contrast.

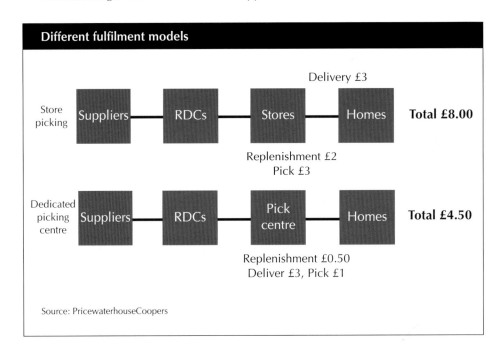

Different fulfilment models

Source: PricewaterhouseCoopers

It is clear that specialised picking centres drive considerable economies from efficient replenishment and picking — but they require investment. However, there is still a cost involved in taking over order picking and home delivery — traditionally carried out by customers. The grocery example also shows interesting contrasts between traditional retailers and dedicated e-tailers. The costs of maintaining a network of stores is largely fixed — and home deliveries simply add cost elsewhere.

For e-tailers, there is no fixed cost of stores. For typical supermarkets, store operations costs typically account for 15% of sales. Based on an average order size of £50, the typical fulfilment cost of £4.50 represents 9% of sales — a clear saving, and an attractive proposition as an alternative to store-based sales. Order sizes of as little as £30 could be delivered for the same cost as maintaining a store network.

So, even in grocery, the economics of e-tailing and home delivery look attractive. However, this demand channel does face challenges: in that it requires access to the home to avoid leaving goods on the doorstep, there is a lack of scale to get economies in buying and fulfilment; and there is a lack of established brands.

Scale is crucial for the economies of both delivery and buying. Although current grocery firms are burdened with an expensive network of stores, new start-ups face years of uncertainty and losses before establishing an economic customer base.

NEW RETAIL BUSINESS MODELS

New models of retail organisations have emerged due to the enabling technology. Many may simply be part of a transition phase — but some may be a template for the future.

There are, of course, e-tailers who operate exclusively on-line. Current retailers are also diversifying into on-line selling. In addition, some manufacturers have seized the opportunity to sell direct to consumers. Beyond these, as the following examples show, the possible operating models are diverse.

Commission-based infomediary

The Web is an excellent medium for providing information — and this business model builds on that strength. These organisations help the consumer choose, by providing selection criteria to narrow the search and then produce information, lists of prices and merchants that can supply the products.

For consumers, the service eliminates the time-consuming process of researching and shopping around. For retailers, it provides a new demand channel — but they are usually fully responsible for fulfilling the customer order. The infomediary then charges a commission on the sale — it is estimated that such charges will be around 8% of sales price.

> **Case study: Autobytel and Brandwise**
>
> Autobytel provides a service to car buyers. It provides information to help in choosing price lists, press reports, specifications, running cost information etc. It then passes purchase orders on to a local dealer, taking a cut of the purchase price. It also contains links to associated services such as insurance, financing and servicing.
>
> Brandwise is an on-line service set up in September 1999 in the US. It started with large home appliances, providing product testing reports and consumer feedback as well as product specifications and lists of suitable merchants. A commission is payable whether the purchase is eventually made electronically or not.

Advertising based revenue models

In this case, a Web site gets revenue from selling advertising space — and by providing links to other sites or services. This is usually combined with other functions. It is common with the leading Internet service providers, or portals. Yahoo and AOL's revenues are largely advertising based. They are two of the most popular Web home pages in the world —a space on them is like buying space on a prime time TV show.

Consumer direct

Manufacturers are taking advantage of the new consumer access possibilities to bypass retailers and sell directly to the public. Without setting up stores, they can take the margin enjoyed by the high street merchants. Computer companies have been the leaders in this field — Dell has made a great success out of direct selling. Nike is selling direct to consumers via a Web page.

Sports goods retailers, traditionally high-margin businesses, have expressed concern. In some cases, the potential changes can be radical. A recording artist has traditionally been contracted to a record company, which deals with recording costs, marketing and distribution. With new consumer access channels, greater control is possible. Distribution can be achieved digitally, and other functions outsourced.

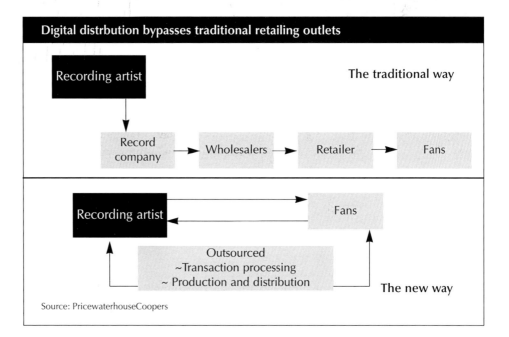

Digital distrbution bypasses traditional retailing outlets

Source: PricewaterhouseCoopers

Auctions

The Internet provides a convenient medium to carry out auctions, with its unrivalled access to a worldwide community of consumers. A number of sites providing this service have been set up.

Case study: Priceline.com, Accompany

Priceline.com is a 'reverse auction' service for airline tickets, new cars and loans. Anybody can enter their requirements, and a price they are prepared to pay — along with credit card details. Priceline then searches for a seller willing to provide: if successful, the sale is made.

Accompany is a San Francisco-based outfit that aims to empower consumers even further. The idea is that a purchaser registers an interest in a particular item — say a Palmtop computer. Accompany then has 72 hours to assemble a group of buyers — 25, 100, 500 at the time. They will then negotiate a discounted bulk buy, and take a small cut, passing the great majority of the savings to consumers.

Airlines have successfully sold tickets in this way. Increasingly anybody from individuals to large corporations can use on-line services to sell goods to the highest bidder.

KEY ISSUES FOR THE CEO

- What are the opportunities for your business from electronic retailing?
- What are the threats to your business from electronic retailing?
- How well placed are you to lead changes, or respond to threats?
- What are the changing requirements and expectations of your customers?
- Can you best develop new services alone, or will partnerships or alliances be required?

Acting with agility — creating the e-factory

INTRODUCTION

"I want this. I want it now. Or else I'll go and get it elsewhere!" Meeting this demand is the age-old challenge of manufacturers and retailers everywhere.

But in today's world — where technology is changing the way we look at everything — ignoring customers' demands is a recipe for disaster. Put simply, manufacturers need to rethink the way their products are made. The advent of e-business is making it all the more pressing.

So, imagine a more perfect world where all products are individually matched to what the consumer wants. Now imagine that these products can be delivered in minutes of their decision to buy. And to make it a harder test of the imagination, that these products contain a mix of components and materials, electronic and mechanical, metallic and plastic parts.

This chapters looks at such scenarios, and the pressures and opportunities that e-business presents to the manufacturing sector. It looks as how a supply chain can be configured to satisfy such demands and what the manufacturing process will look like.

The demands on manufacturers are increasing. Of prime importance is the need to respond to customers more quickly. This creates a pressure for shorter delivery lead times and shorter product life cycles. At the same time, customers are becoming more demanding. The manufacturer must interact closely with its customers and be prepared to offer a greater choice of products.

This may force it to change its processes to allow smaller batch production, with reduced economies of scale, and mass customisation, with similar products being individually tailored before they reach the customer.

If one sets this against a background of continuing market changes, such as globalisation, the emergence of the developing world and the ease of foreign investment, then the outlook for manufacturing companies is one of enormous change.

Market trends

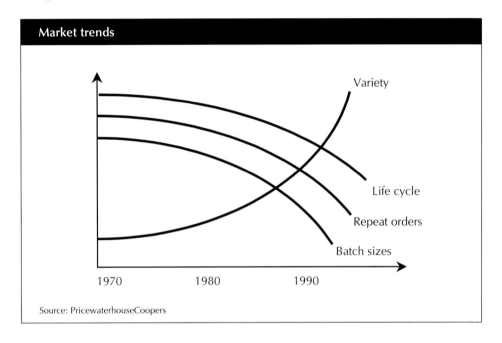

Source: PricewaterhouseCoopers

Typical responses to these issues will range from major reviews of a company's worldwide infrastructure to bringing the performance of individual facilities in line with the demands of e-business.

To help them decide the right course of action for their business, directors should be asking themselves a series of key questions.
- How radically different could products be manufactured within the context of e-business?
- How can manufacturing help differentiate the business?
- How does one ensure acceptable returns on investment in manufacturing capability?
- How can one exploit the manufacturing capabilities of other organisations?
- What will an e-factory look like?
- When will it be necessary to respond to changes driven by e-business?
- Will e-business create a manufacturing revolution or is it a question of evolution?

THE MANUFACTURING REVOLUTION

Just how radically different might the manufacturing infrastructure be in the future?

The scenario at the start of this chapter may seem extreme, but there is already evidence to suggest that those firms that can satisfy such specific consumer wishes in relatively short time-scales are increasing their market share. For example, market demand for customisation has driven postponed assembly strategies in the personal computer industry to the point where some do not start assembly until a firm order is received, at which time a rapid response is triggered.

So, what could the manufacturing response to this scenario look like? It is unlikely that a centralised manufacturing set-up, with one global facility, could satisfy the delivery requirements, even with the efficient logistics now available.

How decentralised and local could manufacturing facilities become? Could there be a fully flexible, make-anything-to-order factory in each major town to satisfy all the local needs? This would create a cottage manufacturing industry, suggesting a shift towards self-sufficiency at a town level in some markets.

More likely will be the creation of products and related facilities that allow very late customisation close to the point of consumption. Likely examples of such changes will include the home assembly of personal computers and dealers finalising the assembly of cars, a topic often discussed in automotive industry forums.

The idea of home manufacture or assembly is not so new. For many years, furniture has been self assembled in the home to a consumer specification, a simple example being the positioning of shelves in a bookcase. What the customer has bought is the required components and the knowledge to convert them into a custom product. Home bread-making machines, knitting machines and home brew kits are all further examples of how stages of manufacture can be carried out in the home of the consumer.

For markets in which data is the prime purchase, postponed manufacture in the home will soon be a reality. On-line bookstores intend their customers to download material from the Internet and print them on a home printer. The music industry is considering a similar concept with consumers downloading music and applying already developed technology to burn their own CDs.

Common truths

- The overall time to produce a custom product (current or new in response to a specific demand) will be a defining factor in competitiveness.
- All stages of the manufacturing process will need to be exceedingly responsive — the increasing risk of redundancy of product will drive stock levels of materials, components, assemblies to all-time lows.
- Postponed assembly and customisation will prevail and the finishing stages of manufacture will move closer to the customer.
- High levels of modularity in product and process design will be a key factor in enabling the required response.

Focusing for the future

Heads of businesses need to ask themselves: what is the significance of manufacturing in their business? To be a market leader in the e-business world will require businesses to be excellent, or to acquire excellence in every key activity.

The alternative is extinction. It is not enough to think of manufacturing as a single competence. When asking "at what do we need to excel?" one must recognise that excellence must be retained internally for some aspects of manufacturing, such as the manufacture of certain product families or key steps in the manufacturing process, while, for others, excellence may be acquired from other parties.

The challenge of achieving an acceptable return on investment becomes increasingly difficult as manufacturers are faced with decreasing product lifecycles, the rapid introduction of replacement products, and process technologies that have unpredictable futures in established markets.

Investment decisions will be influenced to a greater extent than ever by the potential whims of consumers and the rate of product and process innovation.

In the car industry, this challenge was a big one for suppliers in the late 1980s and into the 1990s that also wanted to reduce exposure to volume volatility. In one major supplier, the approach taken to reduce the risks associated with assets was to form a range of different relationships with some current and some new suppliers. These took on certain aspects of the traditionally in-house manufacturing process.

These suppliers were able to reduce the overall manufacturing asset risk by a variety of means. These included the use of manufacturing assets to supply into other customers, the use of more relevant process technology, and better performance in processes that were their prime focus. The major supplier retained final assembly processes for most products, as well as some key manufacturing processes for components that helped differentiate their products within the market.

Products and processes can be categorised in two ways when deciding whether they are candidates for an alternative approach to manufacture and supply.

First, what is the strategic importance of this product or process to the business?

Second, how competitive is the business in respect of the process or manufacture of the product?

Clearly, a strategically important product which one produces more effectively than most is likely to be kept in-house. A standard process in which one's

A framework for capabilities development and selection

Source: PricewaterhouseCoopers

performance is mediocre would make a good candidate for the consideration of other options, such as sub-contracting or outsourcing.

By focusing on key elements of the manufacturing process, and not having to invest management attention where payback is limited, manufacturing capability is likely to improve. This may be to the point where excellent capability in the manufacture of a particular component could help differentiate the business in the market place. For example, without the distraction of less reliable processes, attention can be focused and invested in the processes that produce the more critical components, enhancing process capability and thereby improving product quality and reliability.

The impact of manufacturing on all key aspects of business performance further emphasises the need to get it right.

The impact of manufacturing on business performance			
Cost	Cash	Customer	Market satisfaction
• Direct labour productivity • Production capacity utilisation • Optimisation of economies of scale	• Work in progress • Waste/scrap/ rework • Asset realisation • Manufacturing lead times	• Product quality • Delivery time	• Efficiency improvements provide capacity without capital • Competitive advantage through lower unit cost
Source: PricewaterhouseCoopers			

Networks of agile factories

No matter what the outcome in terms of manufacturing configuration, it is clear that different factories will need to work together effectively to satisfy new, challenging customer requirements. This is one way in which e-business technology will help the overall manufacturing process to become more closely co-ordinated and less bureaucratic in its operation.

One master production schedule could be posted by the customer organisation and, via a supplier bill of material, suppliers could in turn access the areas of the master production schedule relevant to them. This removes the need for tier one suppliers to place orders on tier two suppliers (and so on) and suppliers would not need to produce a separate master production schedule of their own.

Such a synchronised approach would minimise interface costs and create the potential for greatly reduced stock levels in the supply chain (subject to achieving the required manufacturing responsiveness).

The return to functional factories

In asset intensive manufacturing, the network could consist of single capability factories working closely together with an assembler to satisfy end-customer requirements. Each would achieve a good return on assets by serving a range of assemblers of different products in different markets.

To operate efficiently this network would require excellent logistics performance or co-location. One could envisage a group of feeder factories, each with a single capability, surrounded by a range of assemblers fed by them. Internalising this thinking to one business, one is practically describing a traditional factory with functional departments.

Are we going full circle? In some respects, yes, but effective use of assets in the future may well only be achieved if scale is sought across different business sectors. This will especially be the case for large investments where business sectors can only foresee a market life for an asset of, say, 12 to 18 months, thereby making individual asset ownership financially unfeasible.

AGILE FACTORIES

The ability to create truly agile, integrated factories will dictate the degree to which the network approach becomes unnecessary.

What will an agile factory look like? There are two key dimensions to agility: responsiveness and configurability.

Responsiveness is the factory's ability to produce what is required quickly and effectively. This focuses on the need to respond quickly to customers.

Configurability is the ability of the factory to re-configure to produce a significantly different product without incurring excessive cost or needing large capital investment. This focuses on the need to meet return on investment targets.

Responsiveness

The ultimately responsive factory can be defined as one that can satisfy customers within the required lead time, with zero stock and competitive returns.

A common misconception is that to achieve such a performance requires major capital investment. Many businesses have made large steps towards meeting these goals by changing the way in which current resources are applied and managed.

Traditionally, in many industries, cost efficiency has been a prime manufacturing driver. It is this fact that has led to the configuration of assets and the management approach. Manufacturing resources have been measured in terms of efficiency and this has driven the behaviour of operators and management.

Many examples exist of just-in-time manufacturing set-ups that have been created from existing asset bases and have delivered completely different performance. These have involved changes in structure, layout, procedures, planning, roles and supplier relationships.

Even in many industries traditionally considered to be inflexible due to their asset base, agile manufacturing performance has been achieved. This has largely been done through empowering the staff — by taking a new view of what the business requires of them and how they can deliver it.

Technology, clearly, can play a significant part in creating agile factories. The choice of manufacturing technology for new agile facilities should ultimately be driven by the demand pattern (mix, average demand and variability) and the required response times. It is important to note, however, that decreasing product lifecycles and the rate at which technology is developing ensure that returns on the asset targets will be demanding and a longer-term view of asset usefulness will be required for investment decisions.

A conceptual framework for agile manufacturing	
Generic features model	• Integrated enterprises • Human networking organisation • Enterprises based on natural grounds • Increased competencies of all people • Focus on core competencies • Virtual corporations • An environment supportive of experiments • Multi-skilled and flexible people • Team working • Empowerment of all the people in the enterprise • Knowledge management • Skill and knowledge enhancing technologies • Continuous improvement • Change and risk management
Core concepts	• Strategy to achieve agility • Strategy to exploit agility • Integration of organisation, people and technology • Interdisciplinary design methodology
Competitive foundations	• Continuous change • Rapid response • Quality improvement • Social responsibility • Total customer focus
Requirements for agility	• Flat, flexible organisation • Highly decentralised management • Multi-skilled, flexible labour force • Extremely adaptable strategies and relationships with suppliers and competitors • Complete mastery of lean production and concurrent engineering • Flexible tooling and automation • Deep understanding of customers as individuals • Mastery of continuous change

Configurability

As investment decisions are likely to be considered beyond the immediate product requirement, future asset usefulness will become more important in the decision-making process.

Small-scale equipment
The need for a network approach to manufacturing will be less necessary for some processes and products if capable, small-scale equipment is developed. This needs to deliver the required quality and response for a modest investment — one that can be fully recovered within product lifecycles.

Six essential conditions for agility empowerment

- Employees must be properly trained. There is no sense in giving authority without the skills to exercise it effectively. The best companies will have employees with the deepest knowledge.
- There needs to be a shared vision. An organisation cannot move at speed towards a goal until all employees understand where the goal is. Visions should set targets that excite people to want to reach them.
- There needs to be a whole new set of values for rapid culture change. New standards of behaviour and beliefs are required to promote the rapid culture changes needed. Letting an existing culture determine the terms and conditions of change will lead to failure in improving performance.
- The reward system needs to be re-structured so that employers feel that they will benefit from working in a more agile environment. Reward solely on contribution and performance.
- Managers must trust employees. Management ethics must be seen as open, fair and consistent. Empowerment requires a faith that employees will do the right thing.
- The overall culture of the organisation must encourage risk taking. Employees must feel that by taking risks they will not be exposing themselves to punishments for failure. Only by allowing everyone to take risks will organisations evolve at the necessary pace.

Simple assets

The alternative to large capital investment could be a component approach to building a manufacturing process. This is easiest to envisage in terms of single operation machine tools positioned in sequence (eg turn radius, radius end, mill flat, coat powder, bake coating, machine face), with each step of the process being performed on a free-standing machine.

Such an approach can be found in practice today (often referred to as Nagare cells), advantages being simplicity of configuration to new requirements, low maintenance costs, and ease of training.

Alternative uses

Full recovery of investment in manufacturing assets is not a new challenge. Often a business will go out and seek alternative markets it could serve with an under-utilised asset. An example of this is the automated deep drawing facility used to produce missile rocket motor cases. The demand for this product dropped with the end of the Cold War and the business needed to find new demand; in the end it was used to produce extinguisher tubes.

A more optimal position would be to use the same asset to manufacture replacement products for the current range into the same market; this thinking would obviously be aided by a robust medium-term product plan.

Where such asset solutions are not technically or financially viable, the need is to again consider the degree to which a manufacturing network could form part of the overall solution.

The solution to the agility challenge will necessarily vary by industry and within industries. The relevance of a range of approaches to different industries is under increasing scrutiny. Examples of possible applications for these solutions include small-scale responsive chemical plant and easily re-configurable electronic assembly plant.

E-nabler

Whatever the solution for a particular business, probably a hybrid of those individual solutions discussed, the information technology now available will enable the linking and synchronising of the associated elements.

E-BUSINESS AND MANUFACTURING CAPABILITY

One major questions that all manufacturers need to know — "When will it be necessary to respond to the changes driven by e-business?" — unfortunately has no simple or single answer. The answer, and the all important "how to?", will vary greatly by industry and market sector.

However, there are a number of factors that can be considered in trying to answer this question, such as:
- Consumer influence/proximity
- Product lifecycle
- Technology lifecycle

Trends in the adoption of new manufacturing thinking suggest that businesses with closer links to consumers will change first in response to the demands and possibilities of e-business.

Fashion, new technology and more demanding customers drive the product lifecycle. New product and process innovation and ever-increasing levels of competition in turn drive the need to find and apply new manufacturing technologies.

By this logic, the earliest adopters of responses to e-business issues will be those:
- Whose customers want customised products and they want them first and now.
- That operate in markets where competitiveness can be clearly related to new product innovation.
- That must apply new process technology to deliver the levels of performance required.

As a consequence, these will be the players who lead the field in manufacturing agility, in the form of responsiveness (short term) and configurability (medium and longer term).

ADOPTING MANUFACTURING RESPONSES TO E-BUSINESS

Businesses that feed these early adopters are likely to feel insulated from the same pressures due to their upstream position in the supply chain. This is a key factor in the later adoption of the required changes.

Those that do adopt early, however, will be in a strong position to be preferred suppliers as the need to adopt becomes more critical over time. Currently, e-business, and the required responses, form part of a "must-do-to-be-in-business" strategy for some and present an excellent opportunity to differentiate for others. Ultimately, however, all will have responded thoroughly to the e-business changes, or they will be on the road to extinction.

The correlation between getting new products to market and business growth is becoming increasingly robust as more data is collected to test it.

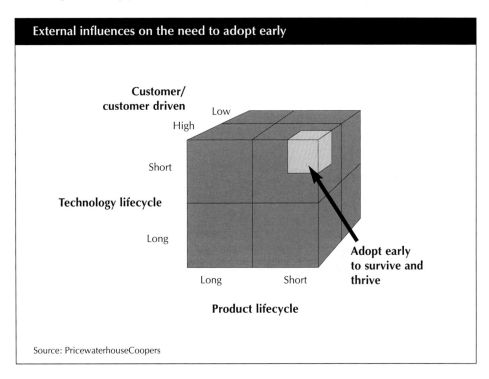

External influences on the need to adopt early

Source: PricewaterhouseCoopers

The time taken to get a product to market is a key ingredient to such success. For example, the benefits of manufacturing agility, both internally and in a network, are demonstrated by the speed at which new products are at full volume production in some car manufacturers.

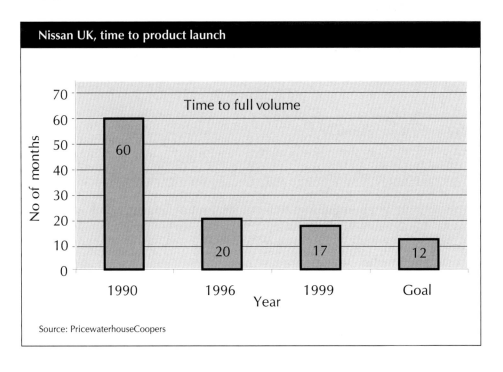

Nissan UK, time to product launch

Source: PricewaterhouseCoopers

Rapid prototyping experts

As manufacturing capabilities become more widely distributed, the need will exist for specialists that have the facility to produce prototype products. Specialism will mean having the range of manufacturing capabilities required by a target prototype market and the ability to turn requests around quickly.

Relationships with customers will be a key factor in such businesses, which will probably serve competitors in given markets so that asset utilisation is maximised and the operation is financially viable.

E-BUSINESS AND MANUFACTURING: REVOLUTION OR E-VOLUTION?

So what does the future hold? Revolution or e-volution? To understand where manufacturing stands today, it is important to consider the changes in manufacturing during the 20th century and put the changes discussed in this chapter into that context.

Responsive manufacturing: a time line from mass production onwards

Mass production	MRP	CIM	JIT	BPR	Lean production	?
1920	1970	1980		1990	Today	tomorrow

Some of tomorrow's challenges come through the boardroom
- e-business
- globalisation of industries and markets
- increasing number of mergers, acquisitions and disposals
- changing mix of strategic partnerships and outsourcing
- excess capacity in many industries
- collapsing product life cycles
- real time agility
- consumer adoption rate of new technology
- need to re-configure assets quickly

Old solutions for manufacturing do not match up to this developing new world.

Source: PricewaterhouseCoopers

To understand whether this means revolution, one must consider some of the required changes within the business.

All manufacturing businesses must come to terms with these changes, and those that have not yet started are clearly faced with a revolution. In others that have the urgency to adopt and are therefore already en route, the process is more evolutionary. The type of journey largely depends on the starting point.

It is clear that a significant element of the new world will be the roles which people play. This may be the better indicator of whether the change will be evolutionary or revolutionary.

Within the manufacturing context, the ability to respond and re-invent to new and changing requirements is becoming a core competence in its own right.

Creating competitive advantage through manufacturing

Client needs	Actions	Activities	Measures
• Shorter lead times	• Process re-engineering • Set up focused factories	• Self-directed terms • Multi-skilling • Increased autonomy • Reduced span of control	• Lead time
• Reduced time to market	• Improved new product introduction processes • Simultaneous engineering	• Install new processes for new product introduction and project management	• Time to market • Time to full volume • % of new products in range • Contribution from new products
• Improved response to customer requirements	• Synchronisation • Pull scheduling • Improved S&OP	• One piece flow • Kanbans • Local control boards	• On time in full • Customer satisfaction
• Cost reduction	• Yield improvement • Lean processes — elimination of non-value added activities	• Process re-engineering • JIT/Kaizen • Target costing and ABC analysis • Work standardisation	• Yield improvement • First time pass rate • Value added per employee • Return on capital employed
• Increased product variety	• Mass customisation	• New run strategies • Modular product build • Design for customisation	• Sales variety
• Improved product quality /performance	• Defect elimination • Design for manufacture	• Statistical process control • 6 sigma quality programmes	• Defect measures • Reliability • Warranty costs
• Improved customer intimacy	• Process re-engineering • Change management	• New ways of working • Culture change	• Customer satisfaction • Customer service • Workforce can articulate the new vision

KEY ISSUES FOR THE CEO

E-business will create the need to rethink the way in which products are manufactured. This means manufacturing has to consider the following factors.

- What will agility mean to manufacturing in your industry?
- How radically different could products be manufactured in the context of e-business?
- How can manufacturing help differentiate the business by responding to e-business driven changes and leveraging e-business capabilities?
- How does one ensure acceptable returns on investment in manufacturing capability?
- How can one exploit the manufacturing capabilities of other organisations?
- When must manufacturing respond to e-business driven changes?

Living with the enemy — working with service partners

INTRODUCTION

Fragmentation and narrow service offerings have been the traditional characteristics of the logistics marketplace. Recently, logistics operators have sought to add more value to their customers, in order to move away from their perception as a commodity service. They have been extending their service scope, creating more regional and global infrastructures, creating innovative commercial relationships and simply improving their processes.

The world of the logistics service provider (LSP) has been changing for several years. These companies have been responding to the needs of their customers, which have largely withdrawn from their non-core activities, leaving room for the LSPs to widen their scope.

Technology advances have been instrumental to this change, but the real electronic business onslaught is still just around the corner. How will it affect the LSPs, and what will they have to do to compete? This chapter answers these questions.

The development of the market

The concept of third-party logistics services is not new. Companies that perform part or all of another organisation's supply chain activities for a fee have been around for generations, as far back as the trading houses and service organisations which used to be prevalent in Europe and the Far East. In recent years, the popularity of these companies, now commonly called logistics service providers or LSPs, has grown as shippers have begun to recognise the benefits of lower investment and operating costs and their ability to use the external marketplace to get best practice processes, more flexibility and operating synergies.

However, the highest demand for outsourced service provision traditionally resides in warehousing and transportation. Until the last five years, there has been relatively little growth in the outsourcing of other supply chain functions.

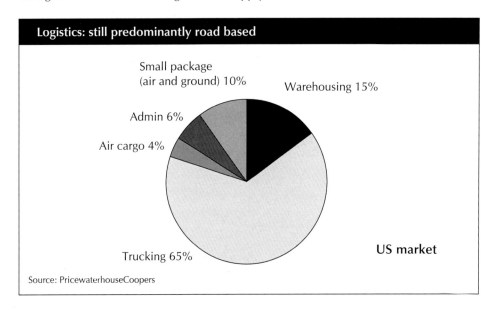

Logistics: still predominantly road based

Small package (air and ground) 10%
Warehousing 15%
Admin 6%
Air cargo 4%
Trucking 65%
US market

Source: PricewaterhouseCoopers

Over the last few years, examples of adding value elsewhere in the supply chain have begun to emerge.

- Pre-assembly of modular components for the automotive industry is often carried out by logistics suppliers.
- Call centre management for order handling is starting to be seen as non-core within a number of sectors, such as pharmaceuticals.
- Some providers are starting to offer to take title to inventory, particularly where they are able to leverage lower funding costs than their customers.
- One company in the UK has recently become the country's second-largest provider of debt factoring services as a result of a contract with a major multi-national chemicals organisation.
- UPS worldwide logistics provides a professional tuning service for Fender guitars before delivery to retail outlets.

EXTENDED LOGISTICS OUTSOURCING

Inroads into supply chain processes outside the traditional core skills base of these providers are set to continue.

The recent PricewaterhouseCoopers European supply chain survey reviewed the extent to which large manufacturing and retailing organisations are sharing supply chain management and demand management activities now, and the extent to which they anticipate doing so in five years' time. The results are shown in the following chart.

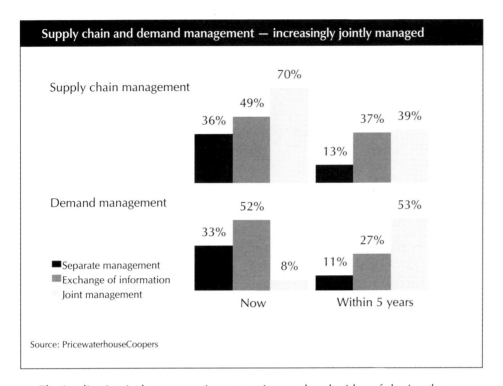

Supply chain and demand management — increasingly jointly managed

Source: PricewaterhouseCoopers

The implication is that companies are getting used to the idea of sharing the management of vital supply chain elements. In spite of the complexity of these activities, and the impact they have on business performance, 40% to 50% of European manufacturing companies believe that those activities will be jointly managed (either in-house or outsourced) within five years. A new concept is emerging — extended logistics.

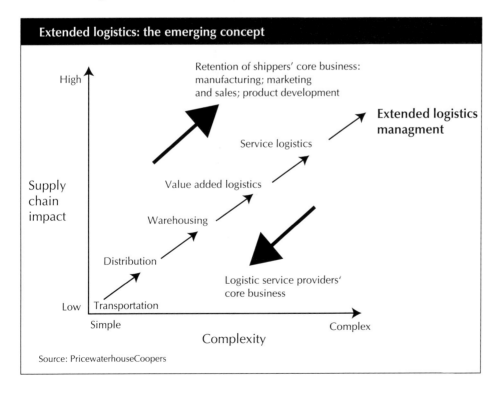

Extended logistics: the emerging concept

Source: PricewaterhouseCoopers

Clearly, the opportunity for logistics suppliers to manage supply chain processes other than transport and warehousing will be highly sector (and organisation) specific. To some, purchasing may be a core business process not to be outsourced (for example, grocery retail), and to others (for example, certain consumer packaged goods brand owners) manufacturing is a non-value adding process that could logically be given to a third party.

Nonetheless, the extended logistics proposition is a valid one, assuming a business case can demonstrate that the concept adds more value as a whole than the various alliance partners and sub-contractors could add independently.

So where does e-business fit in with all this? If one acknowledges that e-business consists of both communication and technology elements, then the communication revolution is going to change the LSPs' marketplace, and this will be made possible by the new technology.

TECHNOLOGY AS THE ENABLER

Technology is vital to logistics operators, both for optimising their core supply chain activities and linking with their customers' supply chain planning and execution systems.

Planning tools

Supply chain network design software is a key tool in this area, particularly where customers have not invested in their own strategic and tactical planning systems and where benefits are clearly obtainable from the rationalisation or redesign of manufacturing and distribution networks.

Also, simulation software in a post-merger scenario can be used to help carry out an integrated analysis of suppliers, production, storage and transportation, by time, cost and service level, split by product.

This represents powerful leverage for LSPs that have the capability to implement at the back end of the planning process, identifying cost savings for customers.

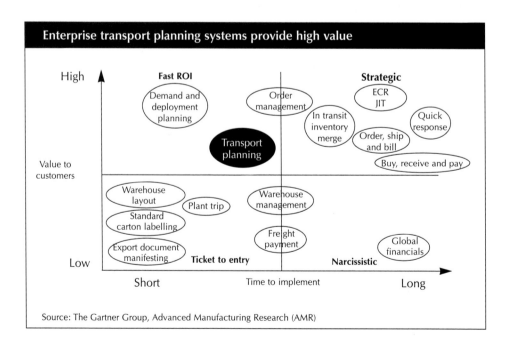

Enterprise transport planning systems provide high value

Source: The Gartner Group, Advanced Manufacturing Research (AMR)

Executional tools

Given the current focus on transport and warehousing, the two key executional tools are WMS (warehouse management systems) and TMS (transportation management systems). Best of breed applications often provide better functionality than modules within enterprise-wide systems, providing more opportunity to optimise the cost/service mix, and therefore for LSPs to add value for their customers.

These tools have suffered from the problem of conflicting goals, with transport managers trying to optimise load planning before releasing orders to the distribution manager, who needs early visibility of orders to optimise productivity.

This conflict is exacerbated when these systems are linked to other executional tools, such as inventory management, order management, manufacturing and supplier management systems.

However, order entry, transportation management and warehouse management systems are becoming much more tightly integrated and the benefits are realised through reduced costs, enhanced productivity and, subsequently, improved customer satisfaction. Executional software has grown explosively in recent years, and the Gartner Group and Advanced Manufacturing Research (AMR) have recognised these transport and warehousing systems, in particular, as having a high potential for fast returns on investment.

Track and trace systems

The major parcels integrators are the clear market leaders in track and trace systems. They maintain that consignment and vehicle tracking provide their unique source of competitive advantage.

Technology can provide business customers with direct access to tracking systems, allowing direct visibility of consignments at any part in the transportation process. They can offer exception-based management reporting for customers, who will not generally want to continuously monitor all their inbound product flows. This provides the opportunity for real-time dynamic scheduling within production processes.

Integration with customers' supply chain systems

The tools described above all represent point solutions that logistics service providers employ to improve service offerings to customers. But there has been a recent explosion of enterprise-wide resource planning (ERP) transaction systems implementations by major manufacturers and retailers. This, together with the rapidly expanding use of strategic advanced planning and scheduling (APS) tools, means there is also a need for logistics suppliers to ensure their offerings are compatible — so enhancing the inherent functionality of these major packages. There are two clear advantages of ensuring effective systems integration. The first is to enhance customer buy-in to joint solutions and to improve and deepen the account relationship. The second is the foundation it can provide for extended logistics outsourcing.

A good example of technology taking the LSP role further is found with APS applications. Understanding and linking with a customer's supply chain wide planning applications is, perhaps, the ultimate move of logistics service providers (with alliance partners if appropriate) into the supply and demand planning areas.

A typical response is shown in the following chart.

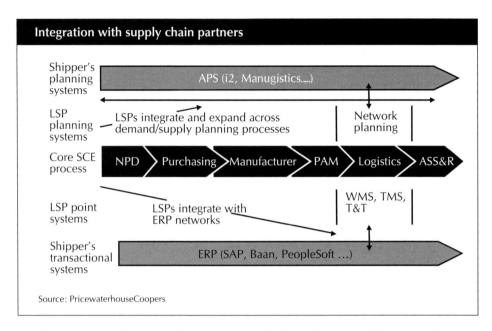

Integration with supply chain partners

Shipper's planning systems — APS (i2, Manugistics.....)

LSP planning systems — LSPs integrate and expand across demand/supply planning processes — Network planning

Core SCE process — NPD > Purchasing > Manufacturer > PAM > Logistics > ASS&R

LSP point systems — LSPs integrate with ERP networks — WMS, TMS, T&T

Shipper's transactional systems — ERP (SAP, Baan, PeopleSoft ...)

Source: PricewaterhouseCoopers

There is no doubt that the third-party extended logistics proposition is a valid one, and all indications are that the outsourcing trend is set to accelerate across other supply chain processes.

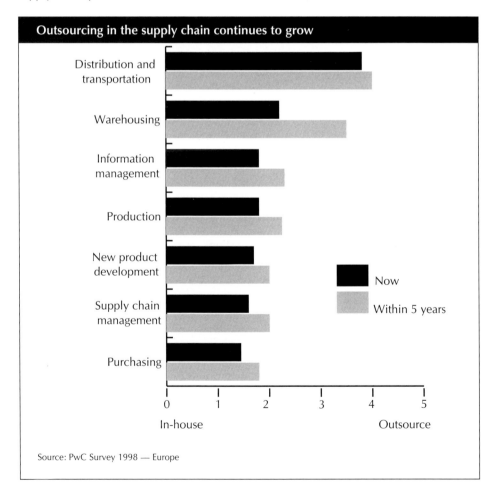

Outsourcing in the supply chain continues to grow

Distribution and transportation

Warehousing

Information management

Production

New product development

Supply chain management

Purchasing

Now

Within 5 years

0   1   2   3   4   5

In-house   Outsource

Source: PwC Survey 1998 — Europe

THE IMPACT OF E-BUSINESS

The logistics market has been evolving at pace for several years, and these potential developments are an extension of that. Customer needs are changing as is technology. Logistics operators need to change in step and then move ahead — there's nothing new about that.

But that is not all that is changing. E-business is about more than just technology. Technology is allowing the market to change, giving it radically new means of communication and data management opportunities. Logistics operators need to anticipate the new environment in which they will do battle and manage information, not assets.

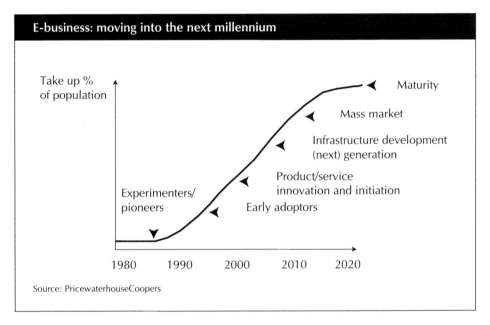

E-business: moving into the next millennium

Source: PricewaterhouseCoopers

E-business will achieve critical mass in the next decade. It will affect every industry and revolutionise many — ignoring it will not be an option.

In terms of supply chains, there will four main ways in which the impact of e-business occurs:

- Reducing physical assets (dematerialisation).
- Eliminating steps in the supply chain (disintermediation).
- Creating extended enterprises (deverticalisation).
- Increasing product development, by enabling strategies to focus on core areas, increase offerings and introduce postponement?

Dematerialisation

The vision for electronic supply chains is one of products moving swiftly along transparent paths with perfect visibility of data from end-to-end.

In these circumstances, shippers will seek flexibility and responsiveness. Traditional areas of high fixed cost, such as warehouses, inventory and, to some extent, manufacturing plant, will start to become more of a liability than an asset.

Logistics service activities will become more integrated with core business processes, and providers will add value to their customers by bringing to bear skills in areas such as cross-docking and dynamic transport scheduling.

Disintermediation

Particularly in business-to-consumer trade, the new market channel created by the Internet has the potential to eliminate wholesalers and retailers as manufacturers/brand owners sell directly to the consumer.

The pace at which this trend evolves will vary widely by sector and geography, and in many the channel conflicts will be difficult to overcome.

However, responding to this need will fundamentally change the economics of the distribution process. Logistics providers wishing to compete in this evolving market will need to respond to the challenges of short lead times, small consignments and multiple drop delivery networks.

Deverticalisation

The increase in use of electronic channels to market, and the resultant increase in importance of brand, is likely to focus the attention of brand owners on the core processes of innovation, product development and brand lifecycle management. After all, switching between suppliers will become much easier for the consumer and other buyers.

As a result, it is likely that demand fulfilment activities will be outsourced. This will enhance the rate of growth of the core market for logistics suppliers. Opportunities may arise for organisations to exploit synergies within sectors and supply chain services on an industry-solution basis.

The manufacturing and logistics processes are likely to be at the forefront of this trend, although potential conflicts of interest will need to be managed, particularly if the industry players believe they compete on the basis of their supply chains.

Product development

As critical mass is reached, and the economic benefits of electronic channels to market become proven across sectors, more and more customer offerings will be developed that extend the concept of electronic commerce.

Case study: NTE

In the business-to-business arena, a typical example is the opportunity to develop a mechanism for linking buyers of vehicle space to carriers looking for back-load opportunities.

The National Transportation Exchange (NTE) in the US has been set up for supply and demand to interact on the Internet. NTE acts as deal broker but also issues contracts and handles payment.

This is a good example of a win-win situation, with shippers picking up low price haulage, carriers generating extra revenue from a fixed cost, and NTE collecting commission.

The Web allows more extensive market reach and better economics than proprietary networks. A future scenario could be real-time trading, as vehicle drivers use wireless Internet access devices to connect to the NTE Web site enabling a high level of proactivity in predicting demand patterns.

Industry convergence will occur as organisations offer complementary products to their existing customer base. Current examples include supermarkets selling financial services and airlines selling holidays.

Where these products are physical, such as on-line book vendors moving into the gift market, logistics operators that are set up for direct consumer deliveries will continue to benefit.

In other markets, existing distribution structures may collapse completely. Examples include the downloading of music from the Web on to CD-ROM, either by retailers or the end consumer, and creating digital magazines by downloading data on to an electronic medium with the same handling characteristics as traditional paper and print.

IMMEDIATE OPPORTUNITIES

The advent of a new channel to market, and of an economic, real-time communication medium, presents a number of immediate opportunities for service providers.

The clearest opportunity for logistics service providers in the business-to-consumer area is in the rapid increase in home delivery distribution. Bill Gates, chief executive of Microsoft, predicts that a third of all grocery shopping will eventually be conducted on-line, and various estimates put Internet commerce at $200 billion by 2000, and in excess of $400 billion by 2002.

Electronic retailers — e-tailers — fall into three broad categories:

- Local, full-line grocery providers that own their own fulfilment capability (eg Peapod, Streamline).
- National, single category vendors (eg Pet Express, Disney Store).
- Manufacturers (brand managers) that are seeking to disintermediate the delivery channel by eliminating the retailer.

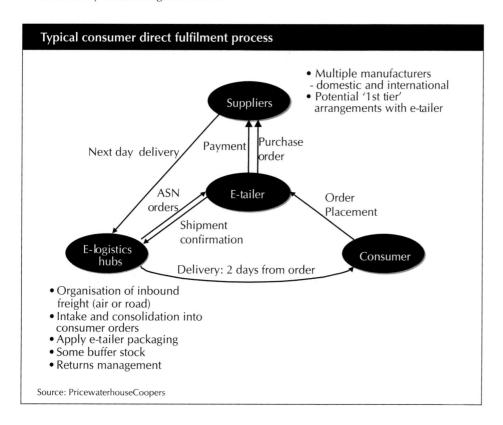

Typical consumer direct fulfilment process

- Multiple manufacturers
  - domestic and international
- Potential '1st tier' arrangements with e-tailer

Suppliers

Next day delivery Payment Purchase order

ASN orders E-tailer Order Placement

Shipment confirmation

E-logistics hubs Delivery: 2 days from order Consumer

- Organisation of inbound freight (air or road)
- Intake and consolidation into consumer orders
- Apply e-tailer packaging
- Some buffer stock
- Returns management

Source: PricewaterhouseCoopers

The previous diagram demonstrates how an LSP might operate the fulfilment service on behalf of the e-tailer.

The lack of a physical high street retail infrastructure and a positive cashflow, are able, in part, to fund premium transportation in such a scenario. But it is clear that providers with large consumer delivery networks already in place (particularly the major parcel integrators) are at an advantage in this area.

The task for those operators that need to build networks is to achieve a critical mass of customers with a similar delivery profile. When network utilisation reaches a critical point and fixed costs are covered, delivery economics start to become attractive enough to dramatically improve the feasibility of the new supply channel.

A response of either using an existing delivery network or developing a new one to serve customers with similar profiles is sufficient for the customer, but it is reactive to the new channel. Logistics operators should be aware of the opportunities to enhance their influence across the total supply chain.

ENHANCING THE LSP ROLE IN THE SUPPLY CHAIN

Extending the influence

The evolution of e-business and globalisation are likely to lead to increased focus on core activities by key players. The subsequent unbundling and re-bundling of traditional activities will create new value chains, although the speed and extent of development of this model will vary greatly by industry sector.

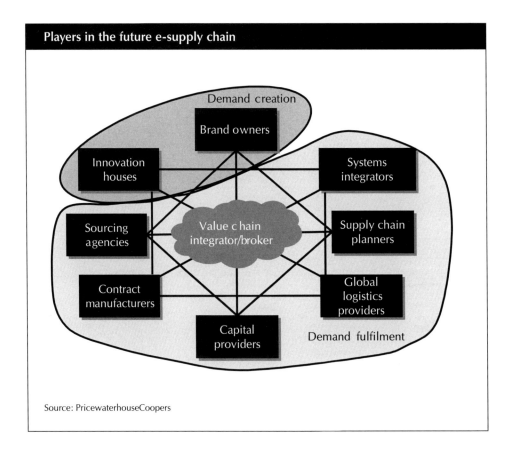

Players in the future e-supply chain

Source: PricewaterhouseCoopers

The above integrator/broker role is a critical one, as it provides the opportunity to shape material and information flows. It wields a significant amount of power and affords opportunities, through enhancing efficiency and effectiveness, for value and profit creation.

In traditional supply chains the power base has, depending on the sector, been with the manufacturer/brand holder or retailer. Although viable enterprises have been set up between other supply chain players, such as LSPs and system integrators, the opportunity for margin growth will be restricted by the influence of the traditional power holders.

One of the key determinants of supply chain influence is control of the consumer interface. Understanding medium-term consumer needs is vital to product development. Understanding immediate buying behaviour is key to effective demand forecasting and supply planning.

Multiple grocery retailers and companies in the high-tech sector, such as Dell, are good examples of how the understanding and application of consumer data can guarantee supply chain control.

So how can LSPs start to extend their influence towards these supply chain processes?

A business-to-consumer example is the extension of order fulfilment to order handling. If the role of LSPs is extended to the front end order management process, through Web hosting, call centre management or both, the LSP gains access to the consumer interface and to data that allows significant supply chain influence.

It provides the ability to capture real demand and, as a consequence, undertake supplier manufacturing scheduling and inventory management. This puts the logistics operator in a prime position to drive improved supply chain efficiency and, through innovative commercial arrangements, to improve margin share.

Skills and experience gained in this new role can be further spun off into three new areas.

- First, the provision of an integrated order handling and fulfilment service to the rapidly growing set of new and innovative e-tailers, whose primary focus during set-up will be on demand creation rather than fulfilment.

- Second, the enhancement of relationships with existing customers by offering expertise in the provision of a complete fulfilment service in an exciting new channel to market.

- Third, an extended order fulfilment service for customers in new geographies. If supported by an effective regional or global logistics structure, logistics operators can claim the role of the traditional distributors that are likely to have become disintermediated by the new channel.

The business-to-consumer market is the most obvious area of changing supply chain structure. However, use of the Internet in a business-to-business context is set to far outstrip business-to-consumer activity in terms of transaction value. So how can service providers make an impact here?

One example is in the automotive sector, where there is huge complexity for manufacturers in the inbound supply chain.

This sector pioneered the concept of first-tier suppliers that act as a focal point for manufacturers and act as managers of inbound supply. The transport management task represents a significant part of this role and, by working with key suppliers, LSPs have the capability to extend their operational reach across the inbound operations for the industry.

Inbound supply chains: opportunities for LSPs

Source: PricewaterhouseCoopers

Also by using their knowledge of the supply base with which they interact, there is a further opportunity for LSPs to add value by speeding up service delivery and act as infomediaries in matching manufacturer demand with component supply.

Early adoption of Internet-based technology is key to exploiting this opportunity to move close to the core supply chain processes of supply planning.

Inbound supply chains are a particularly attractive area for LSPs.

Polarisation in the logistics marketplace

A review of annual reports within any of the major service categories (whether asset, non-asset or parcels based) would traditionally have revealed little basis for differentiation between the major players. New aspirations for LSPs within e-supply chains, however, are likely to lead to a polarisation within the marketplace. Information-based offerings, founded on extended versions of the examples described above, are likely to become distinct from traditional, operations-based offerings.

This does not imply that organisations cannot do both. First-tier providers, that are closer to the core supply chain processes of their customers, will always need the support of second-tier providers, who will focus on operational excellence in their traditional area.

Furthermore, the notion of a second tier necessarily means being under continuous margin pressure. The creation of new supply chains provides opportunities for service providers and contract manufacturers, in particular, to create industry solutions. This is particularly true in sectors where customers are unlikely to see distribution as a source of competitive advantage. The danger is to be caught in the middle. Offering neither industry-leading operational excellence nor value-adding information management

The development of Internet strategies

Process enhancement
- Forecast sharing
- Schedule sharing
- Order status information
- Electronic catalogues
- Remote ATP (available to promise)
- Product data catalogues
- Warranty information
- Order taking
- Inventory visibility
- Capacity visibility
- Load tendering
- Internet EDI (electronic data interchange)
- E-forms
- Training materials
- Frequently asked questions

Market differentiation
- Shared-space collaboration (eg forecasting, promotions, category management, product design, new product introduction, replenishment)
- Exception reporting (eg of inventory shortages, delivery delays)
- Community supply chain metrics

Channel reinvention
- Disintermediation strategies
- Reintermediation strategies
- Shared services

Low   **Sustainable competitive advantage**   High

Source: PricewaterhouseCoopers

services will leave providers with no credible value proposition, and few opportunities to generate growth and shareholder value.

One size does not fit all

So, will the Internet be the silver bullet that allows logistics service providers to take control of the supply chains in which they operate? Clearly not.

Multi-billion dollar brand owners or retailers, as examples, that have the same access to the new technologies, are unlikely to relinquish control of their current or potential consumer interface. Ultimately, the ability of organisations to trade and integrate over the Internet will be driven by the position of power they hold within that particular trading community and Internet strategies will need to be positioned accordingly.

For powerful customers in mature supply chains, proactive LSP strategies are best focused on areas, such as the earlier automotive example, where providers can move towards the core processes of their customer and add value by removing the management burden. In other areas, the LSP may need to comply with customers' demands to use their own information architecture as a shared service environment.

In other cases, such as for new entrant e-tailers with no fulfilment capability, the Internet strategy can be more aggressive, providing LSPs with the capability to dictate business processes, data structure and other standards to other supply chain participants.

What is clear is that supply chain performance will be constrained by the weakest link in the system. Supply chain partners must have the technology to integrate themselves in end-to-end strategies, and enterprises with the capability to integrate using the Internet will find it easier to form strong relationships across the supply chain.

Sector-by-sector strategies will not only be defined by respective supply chain power balances. They will also need to reflect the relative potential of the Internet today.

Previous sections have discussed how LSPs might reposition themselves over time within e-supply chains. There is also a need to match those ambitions with a pragmatic approach to the phased introduction of Internet-enabled services. In the immediate future, the first benefits are to be found in process improvement activities and information sharing across supply chain communities.

An evolutionary approach to the application of Internet strategies may, therefore, be the best route for major customers that are significant power holders within their supply chains. An incremental move towards core supply chain processes builds supply chain presence while maintaining a critical level of trust with the customer.

More revolutionary approaches, for new entrants with immature supply chains, represent much higher risks — picking the winners among start-ups is notoriously difficult. But it does offer the reward of much broader influence to improve supply chain efficiencies and margin, and to build supply chain management experience and skills.

Logistics providers should have a portfolio of Internet strategies that will be sector, geography or even organisation, specific. These will reflect a balance of pro-activity, functionality and speed of implementation.

LEVERAGING SUPPLY CHAIN ALLIANCES

Earlier sections of this chapter have addressed the issue of extended logistics and the many barriers that are associated with its successful pursuit. The previous section has described how e-business could potentially move LSPs towards the centre of the supply chain "Web" by enabling them to manage the systems, planning and physical distribution elements of the demand fulfilment activity.

However, LSPs do not have the skills to move fully into the role of value chain integrator/broker, which might be described as "the control and management of everything within the supply chain of one organisation at strategic, tactical and operational levels".

No single organisation is currently able to manage this entire range of capabilities. However, a review of the skill sets of four major types of organisation involved in the supply chain shows the benefits to be obtained from alliances, and indicates how logistics operators and other players can fulfil this role.

Shippers

Shippers increasingly outsource elements of their supply chains and have frequently lost their skill base in those areas where there is a dependency on the third-party providers. Furthermore, change management, complex forecasting and integrated planning capabilities are often not available to the required level in shipping companies and these remain in the domain of major consultancies and project management firms. However, because they own the customer interface, shippers are

---

Required capabilities for extended logistics management

What do I need?

Operational	• Day-to-day execution of traditional logistics activities as transportation distribution and warehousing • Day-to-day execution of activities that determine the contents of the traditional logistics activities such as sourcing of products
Tactical	• Advanced planning capabilities • Inventory management • Forecasting • Analytical skills and tools • Organisational skills
Strategic	• Knowledge of the logistics market-place and its trends and future structure • Knowledge of logistics structures and how these can benefit the company • Strategic management capabilities for innovation and continuous improvement • A sound strategy with respect to the importance of logistics and supply chain management for the company • Asset management • Assembly/conversion

Source: PricewaterhouseCoopers

---

usually the principal player in the chain and are frequently experts in asset management, assembly and conversion.

System providers

The impact of information and communication technology (ICT) is increasing rapidly in today's business environment. Whether providing point solutions or strategic planning tools, these organisations are helping to facilitate the management of complex value chains.

As well as applications software, a number of companies (such as SAP, IBM, and Oracle) are seeking to provide supply chain-wide inter-operable systems environments. These will allow access for all applications in the supply chain community, so addressing the issue of incompatible legacy systems. Despite their increasing importance, however, software companies still lack the process re-engineering and strategic knowledge necessary to fully realise the benefits of their systems across the chain.

Major consultancy firms

The breadth of the Big Five consultancies' skill sets, particularly in terms of project and change management, strategic vision and systems implementation, places them as potentially strong contenders in the extended logistics area. However, the lack of direct implementation capability means that they would be unable to execute extended logistics management themselves.

Logistics service providers

These companies frequently do not have the strategic skills to be taken seriously at board level in extended logistics discussions. However, they provide strong implementation skills, and possess the infrastructures that are essential to the proposition. They are also the most experienced in running outsourced contracts.

A review of the respective skill sets of these groups demonstrates that combining the best of all worlds becomes a realistic option in the emerging extended logistics marketplace. The vision says that tailor-made solutions will be developed in joint teams combining their strengths to develop a flexible route forward. Strategic alliances and joint ventures will generate objectivity and flexibility for clients.

Extended logistics represents a complex, nascent service and, as such, a number of key issues remain. For example:

- Clients need to be found that are willing to outsource their complete demand fulfilment process, parts of which are still regarded as core competencies.
- The business case needs to demonstrate that sufficient efficiencies can be generated to give all alliance members a suitable return for their contribution.
- Propositions need to be developed case-by-case which provide the right mix of services to clients or industry sectors.

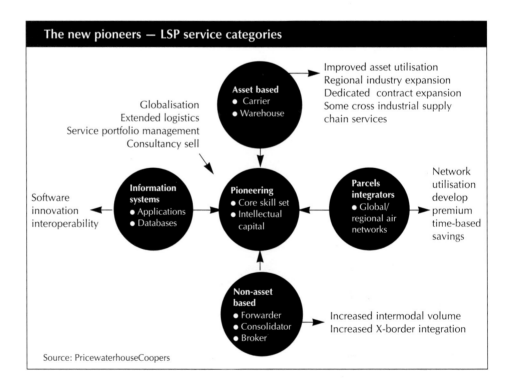

The value chain integrator/broker role may therefore be formed of alliances of companies from the outer "Web".

Speed to market is also essential — once a successful project is in place, the marketplace is likely to follow swiftly, with potentially explosive growth for the successful initiator.

And so the question remains, who will be the early adopter (not necessarily the first mover)? The one that establishes the right mix of skills, proposition and commercial structure to successfully take this exciting new concept to market?

The way forward

The concept of extended logistics is emerging — major manufacturing and retailing organisations are anticipating the outsourcing or joint management of their core demand and supply chain planning processes.

Leading edge logistics providers, as well as consolidating in their core skill areas, are developing new capabilities as portfolio managers, intellectual capital providers and alliance/relationship builders. They are increasingly willing to invest in information, rather than asset, based competencies that will move them closer to their customers' core supply chain processes.

Enabling technologies, to date, have allowed logistics providers to add value through best of breed point solutions within the logistics function, and also through compatibility with the ERP and APS systems being implemented widely by their customer base.

In the new millennium, the Internet will offer some immediate opportunities, particularly in the business-to-consumer area, with the anticipated rapid increase in home deliveries.

An early adopter approach to the new technology will give further opportunities for providers to dramatically enhance their role in the supply chain. In particular, access to the consumer interface, through provision of order management services, for example, yields significant opportunities to drive short and medium- term improvements back through the demand fulfilment process.

This potential needs to be managed. Providing complete supply chain solutions for new entrant e-tailers requires a more aggressive Internet strategy than the more compliant one that will protect and enhance the relationship with a powerful blue chip customer.

The opportunities for logistics providers in the e-supply chain are there. Do they have the competencies to become the integrators of whole industry supply chains as e-business moves businesses from vertical to virtual? Not yet — and not on their own.

Alliances — with consultancies and software providers — appear to provide the key to unlock the potential of extended logistics, and the improved economics of the e-enabled supply chain should generate the business case.

Revolution? That's not really how this industry develops. But one thing is certain... the rate of evolution is set to accelerate — fast.

KEY ISSUES FOR THE CEO

- As a logistics service provider, what new services or systems must you have to compete in your market in the e-business driven future?
- As a buyer of logistics services, what are you doing that you could outsource, and what would it take for you to be convinced it is a good idea?
- Are your chosen logistics partners geared up for the Information Age?
- How will your systems requirements change?

COMPANY

OM Partners is a solution provider with 15 years of experience in developing and implementing Supply Chain Planning Systems. Beyond the delivery of software, we provide professional assistance from analysis, over implementation to support.

SECTORS

- **Flow Shop** like: Corrugated Board, Metals, Paper, Plastics, Solid Board, Textiles, …

- **Semi Process** like: Animal feed, Chemicals, Dairy, Fertilizers, Food & Beverages, Pharmaceutics, Starch, …

- **Hortica** for horticultural production and optimization of crossings.

PRODUCTS

The OM Partners product range for Supply Chain planning integrates all levels of the planning hierarchy with both interactive and intelligent solutions. These are standard software packages, which can be parametrised to your needs.

OMP Optimization

OMP Optimization (OMP) is our solution for the highest level of Supply Chain planning. It deals with strategic issues like optimal product mix of co- and by-products, sourcing and make-or-buy decisions, warehouse localization and (re)allocation problems.

OMP Master Production Scheduler

OMP Master Production Scheduler (MPS) is an interactive graphical package for Master Planning. Based on sales forecasts and orders from different customer groups in various countries, MPS can take into account machine-, resource- and storage capacities in different plants, material requirements, transportation (truck, train, barge, etc.) and customer specific constraints (batch sizes, buffering policies, etc.). MPS will automatically generate a multi-level finite capacity plan with minimal transportation, manufacturing and storage costs, minimal deviation from inventory and production targets, etc.. MPS also allows for real-time order promising and service level optimization.

OMP Graphical Manufacturing Planner

OMP Graphical Manufacturing Planner (GMP) is OM Partners' solution for detailed scheduling problems. GMP models your production facilities in great detail: set-ups, precedence relationships, tanks and silos, multiple BOMs and resources, batching rules, warehouses, etc. GMP allows to simulate in a mouse-driven windowing environment: drag & drop facilities, order split & merge, graphs and reports built through interactive contents selection, etc. You can monitor inventory and WIP evolution, see the impact of production events and order changes on set-up costs, resource usage, due date performance.

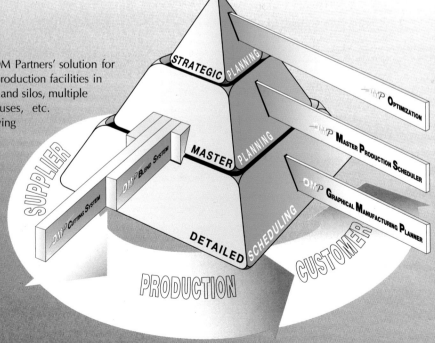

Sophisticated solvers

Intelligent modules exist for optimization problems like cutting, blending, sequencing, cycle planning, ...

OM Partners n.v. • Michielssendreef 40-48 • B-2930 Brasschaat, Belgium
Tel. +32-3-652.03.03 • Fax +32-3-652.07.72 • E-mail: sales@ompartners.com • http://www.ompartners.com

Creating virtual advantage — planning the optimised supply chain

INTRODUCTION

The globalisation of companies and markets, the concentration of fewer, albeit powerful, industry players and rapid technology and process change are becoming the fabric of our lives. High performing companies have been searching for ways to use the power of information and technology to transform the performance of their companies. At the heart of this strategy has been the advent of decision support information systems that can take detailed transaction data and forward plan the organisation through the ever changing seas of business.

Previous chapters have shown how consumer pressures are demanding agility and flexibility from the supply chain, and forcing organisations to work closely together. So how can organisations make the consumer happy in this environment, as well as earn a decent profit?

The answer lies in using the available technology to its full extent. If technology is making demand transparent, then organisations throughout the supply chain need to use that information in a timely, co-ordinated way so that efficiencies are optimised.

This chapter looks at how organisations are using advanced planning and scheduling (APS) systems to help increase the flexibility of their supply chains. It reviews the benefits of collaborative e-planning, which is at the leading edge of APS capabilities and requires a commitment to collaboration across the extended supply chain.

The scope of collaborative e-planning is different from traditional APS initiatives — it includes more than traditional planning, and encompasses order management, customer management and new product introduction processes.

The chapter provides specific examples of how these systems are being used today in an electronic business context and highlights how APS vendors are responding to the challenges of e-business. It also discusses the future for supply chain planning and optimisation, specifically in the areas of collaboration and electronic linkage to external partners, customers and suppliers.

BECOMING DYNAMIC

Having a dynamic supply chain is all about increasing an organisation's ability to deal with variability; that variability can arise from a number of sources, including customers, suppliers and from within the organisation itself.

Optimising where resources are put, where inventories are held, what the structure of the network looks like, and re-assessing these decisions on a regular basis will give organisations a competitive advantage by adding the ability to flex its supply chain's muscles.

For many organisations, a complex supply chain is a reality. Typically, supply chains are built up over time, often through acquisition or market growth. Factors that drive the complexity of a supply chain include:
- Products (numbers of brands/products, promotions, seasonality).
- Customers and channels (customer numbers, customer ordering and delivery types, wholesale/distributor relationships).
- Manufacturing (locations, geographical coverage, process diversity, capacity).
- Logistics (warehouse numbers, locations, size, third party logistics partners).
- Suppliers (supplier numbers, reliability of quality and delivery, relationships).

The complexity of an organisation's supply chain produces a special challenge to the planning function. It has to co-ordinate all of these varied elements to meet defined service levels at lowest costs.

Factors like e-commerce, the Internet, globalisation, and mass customisation continue to change the way in which business is conducted, so supply chain planning has a critical role to play in ensuring the continued success of an organisation.

To satisfy today's consumer, dynamic organisations must operate in a spirit of collaboration with their partners to produce differentiated products and services, delivered through new channels and against new forms of competition.

Effective tactical planning, supported by advanced tools that enable it to be done well, are the keys to success in this environment.

WHAT DOES IT TAKE TO BE GOOD AT SUPPLY CHAIN PLANNING?

Supply chain planning is an umbrella term for a set of business processes that translate strategic objectives into operational instructions. They include, among others:
- Demand planning — what do customers want, and when?
- Supply planning — what inventory does one need where, and when?
- Materials planning — what raw materials are needed and when?
- Production planning — what needs to be made, where and when?
- Transportation planning — what is the best way to deliver it?

How good is your supply chain?

Our supply chain plan is 'time-phased'
A   We don't really plan ahead more than a few days
B   We try to plan a few weeks ahead, but it is often inaccurate
C   We have an integrated set of plans, some strategic for months/years, some tactical for weeks, some at the daily level and below for execution

To re-plan, it takes
A   We don't often re-plan — it takes too long, so we wait for the next planning cycle
B   Days
C   Minutes

When quoting a date to customers
A   We use standard lead times
B   We use the best date available based on knowledge of our organisation's internal constraints and logistics resources
C   Our planning systems provide the best date available based on suppliers' constraints and logistics resources

We tend to find out about material shortages
A   When it is too late and production has stopped
B   Not soon enough but we can replan quickly and this reduces the impact
C   Well in advance and plan accordingly together with our suppliers

We measure manufacturing asset utilisation
A   Each manufacturing facility is measured on asset utilisation
B   Key performance indicators provide a view of all facilities, but adherence to plan is the key measure
C   Key performance indicators show our performance across our extended supply chain, including customers and suppliers

When demand exceeds supply
A   Our back orders increase
B   We usually satisfy the first orders we have received but this sometimes means we upset major customers
C   We allocate the constrained inventory based on the forecast received, forecast accuracy and defined customer priorities

Our customer service levels
A   We try and ensure a service level higher than X% but...
B   We have defined service levels by customer/geography, but we tend to allocate inventory as a safety net
C   We assign target customer service levels based on individual customer priority. Our planning system uses this as one of its planning parameters

New product introduction
A   We regularly miss new product launch dates — it is usually x's fault
B   On major new products, we set up cross-functional teams to ensure we plan accordingly
C   Our new product introduction process is supported by technology which shares information with key suppliers, and gets accurate data from marketing, sales, R&D and operations functions

Predicting demand
A   In our business, it is impossible to plan demand — we usually just respond to orders, but the supply chain isn't really configured for that, and it lets us down
B   We've just started a project to look at this
C   We understand the characteristics of demand; where we need to forecast, we have a one-number consensus built forecast, imputing customer demand and order data to consume/replace the forecast

Answers that are mostly As or Bs show an inability to respond to the inherent complexity of the supply chain and make good tactical decisions. This means that the organisation has a real opportunity to improve the way the supply chain is planned.

What is flexibility?

When defining the flexibility of a supply chain, it is more than just its ability to change from making product 'X' to product 'Y'. Flexibility must be demonstrable in other attributes, including:

Inertia: the ability to change output rate and volume, either up or down to respond to seasonality and other demand changes.

Range: the ability to make and ship multiple products concurrently within the range of current assets and resources.

Frequency: the ability to re-plan, to reduce cycle times, to change from one product to another.

Agility: the ability to reconfigure assets (resources, people, partners) to enhance service or reduce costs.

Power: the ability to develop to meet new challenges, eg new products, new markets, mass customisation.

So how does one achieve a more dynamic supply chain? Dynamic supply chains require both integration and synchronisation.

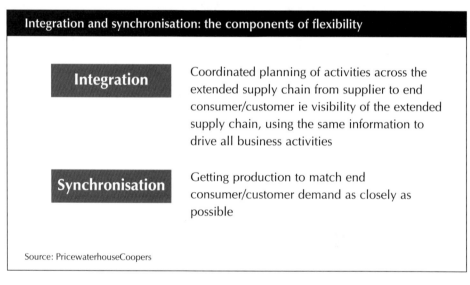

Integration and synchronisation: the components of flexibility

Integration — Coordinated planning of activities across the extended supply chain from supplier to end consumer/customer ie visibility of the extended supply chain, using the same information to drive all business activities

Synchronisation — Getting production to match end consumer/customer demand as closely as possible

Source: PricewaterhouseCoopers

A key requirement for integration is having the data to be able to properly co-ordinate activities, not just internally within one's own organisation, but also with other supply chain partners.

For example, in promising a delivery date to a customer, a truly integrated decision will involve checking the current available inventory in the finished goods warehouse, assessing the future capacity of production to supply that demand, and then ensuring the availability of raw materials to support that production.

This example would require visibility of data such as:

- On-hand inventory.
- In-transit quantities.
- Lead times.
- Production capacities and constraints.
- Supplier plans and inventory.
- Transportation lead times.

Case study: the loudspeaker manufacturer's war cabinet

One US loudspeaker manufacturer has achieved significant levels of improvement from integration and synchronisation throughout its supply networks. The firm recognised that benefits came from reorganising not just the way the managers planned, but where the planners were located and the technology they used.

- It located all the planners in a central "war room" to enable them to optimise the entire system using Manugistics and other specialised planning systems.
- The concept has taken suppliers on to the company's premises. The shipping agent representative sits next to the Amtrak representative and FedEx flight representative.
- The materials planner sits next to the supplier.
- No inventory is carried.
- All raw material components, which are primarily procured from Asia Pacific are stored in the supply chain as inventory on various transportation mechanisms.
- If a run needs to be brought forward, the production planner walks across the "war room" to the transportation planner who may put the raw materials on to, say, a plane or ship, depending on the lead time required.
- This allows for the flexing of the entire supply chain to ensure that the raw materials are delivered to the premises just in time.
- The demand plan is the trigger that activates the "war room" to start functioning.

To meet the delivery date promised, the supply chain needs to be synchronised. All the parties involved (planner, buyer, production shop floor, warehouse operative, transport planner and so on) will need to be acting on the same instructions and basing decisions on the same goal.

APS: EVOLVING OPPORTUNITIES

Percentage of companies satisfied with their forecasting process		
	Low tech forecasts no APS	High tech forecasts with APS
Balanced processes	77%	91%
Ad hoc processes	38%	43%
Source: PricewaterhouseCoopers		

APS is a hot topic. The APS market includes a number of specialist vendors of planning software, including i2 Technologies, Manugistics, Synquest, Logility, Paragon, Chesapeake, LPA, Numetrix and others.

In response to the growing market for APS, enterprise resource planning (ERP)

vendors, such as SAP, Oracle, and Baan, have aggressively developed their own strategies to provide this functionality. They have done this in one of three ways:
- Through alliance partnership arrangements (eg Oracle/ Manugistics).
- Through acquisition (JDE/Numetrix).
- By building from new (SAP-APO).

How do APS systems work?

APS functionality spans from the strategic (such as network optimisation), through tactical (such as supply planning) to the operational levels (such as line scheduling).

How can technology help?

- Manufacturing plant 'X' can produce in one day 500 units of item 'A', or 300 units of item 'B', or a mixture of the two.
- Manufacturing plant 'Y' can produce twice the output of plant 'X' but its products are 20% more expensive.
- Transportation from plant 'X' to the central distribution centre takes two days, whereas transport from plant Y takes only one day.

Such interrelationships of capacity, cost, time and other constraints are even experienced in small, low complexity organisations. Multiply them up to the scale of a global organisation with tens of national operations, hundreds of products, thousands of suppliers and customers and one begins to recognise the need for help from powerful technology.

Most APS systems use mathematical algorithms such as linear programming to identify solutions to complex planning problems that are governed by constraints. Constraints can be any resources that limit the throughput of a supply chain. Examples include production resources, labour, and raw materials. APS systems are particularly well suited to solving the challenges associated with supply chain planning because they:
- Enable the planner to focus on the critical constraints (machine capacity, for example).
- Provide a modelling environment to run different scenarios and 'what-if' analyses.
- Provide decision support — they recommend a course of action, and highlight exceptions.

What benefits can be achieved without APS systems?

It is helpful to understand what can be achieved without using APS technology. Through the 1980s and into the 1990s, the focus of many organisations was on business process improvement. Typically, these process-led change programmes have focused on both the planning and execution processes. They achieved cost reductions, headcount savings and performance improvements by: identifying and reducing non-value added activities; consolidating and rationalising activities; and streamlining business processes, by reducing waste and delays.

For supply chain planning, this has been a valuable approach. For example, a recent survey by PricewaterhouseCoopers identified that in the area of demand planning, many organisations have made significant gains in forecast accuracy by focusing on the process first, and applying technology later.

These results are confirmed by another study by PricewaterhouseCoopers in 1999 that investigated the results of APS implementations. The study found that the benefits from these projects attributable to the new technology alone were between 20% and 30%, depending on the function. The real benefit comes from the combination of process, organisation and technology change.

But there are limits to the level of complexity that a planner can handle without supporting technology. In highly complex situations, the planner will need more than a spreadsheet to be able to develop a good plan.

This is one of the reasons why organisations have turned to APS.

HOW ARE APS SYSTEMS BEING USED TODAY?

As companies strive to improve the performance of their supply chains they have tended to implement APS systems in one of five different ways. These range from the quick and less complex point solutions to leading edge collaborative electronic planning solutions.

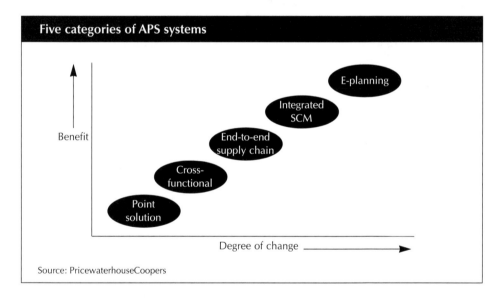

Five categories of APS systems

Source: PricewaterhouseCoopers

APS Point Solutions

This is the starting point for many companies. Typically, a departmental manager realises there is a planning problem and looks for a quick solution to solve it. The problem is perceived to have distinct boundaries. It is usually focused on a single planning function, eg production planning, or transportation planning. There is either no existing technology, or it has limited functionality. Implementations tend to be relatively short, six to nine months, with a good return on investment.

Cross-functional APS

The next way in which APS is being used is to link multiple functions in an organisation to eliminate the silo mentality that traditionally plagued many supply chains.

Typically, the planning challenge cannot be resolved within one functional area of the business, and the APS tool can be used as the catalyst to better integration.

Cross-functional APS represents a more difficult challenge to the point solutions in the first category, but yields higher benefits. Implementation time-scales are generally longer than point solutions because additional effort is required in project management, stakeholder alignment, communications, change management and training.

A good example in this category is demand planning, where the goal is to produce a one number forecast for the business based on achieving consensus across sales, marketing and finance functions.

While cross-functional applications can deliver good results it is only when the business looks to improve the end-to-end supply chain that performance can be really transformed. The final three APS implementation models are gradual extensions of the end-to-end concept.

End-to-end supply chain APS

Here the emphasis is not just on getting one part of the supply chain to operate more effectively, but on synchronising all areas to operate to the same plan, to the same goal.

APS implementation on this scale takes longer, typically 12 to 18 months, and is normally associated with a major change programme involving process redesign and organisational change management.

Conceptually, any business can optimise the end-to-end supply chain but a fundamental prerequisite for success is consistent data. It is rare that a business without a robust ERP system will reap the benefits of this level of implementation.

APS Integrated to supply chain partners

As with end-to-end implementation the objective is to get each part of the supply chain aligned to common goals and objectives. The only difference here being that the scope increases to include suppliers and customers.

Real integration means that several organisations have visibility of the extended supply chain and share information to drive competitive advantage.

This can be the start of collaboration, but is usually fairly limited in scope.

Collaborative e-planning

The final category of APS implementation is the most challenging, but has the highest potential rewards.

Collaborative e-planning represents the leading edge. In addition to sharing data, separate organisations work together to create a plan that reflects the goals and constraints of both parties. Traditionally, trading partners are constantly double guessing what the other party will do in the future — particularly regarding changes to the status quo (price rises, product changes, promotions to name a few). To date each side has had to guess what they think will happen and hedge accordingly.

This hedging, for example stock building, creates unnecessary cost in the supply chain and can lead to poor service.

In the collaborative world organisations will move to a new level of trust and co-operation as they strive to eliminate the remaining causes of supply chain inefficiency.

While building this level of trust is undoubtedly the most challenging aspect of collaboration once achieved, tools are required that support these new workflow models.

The APS vendors have recognised this and have loaded their applications with features that enable them to support joint planning.

Finding what is right: case studies

Getting this right is critical. Going for collaboration when one's internal processes are still functionally oriented is a recipe for disaster. In addition most companies that have achieved success have taken a cautious step-by-step approach to implementing APS tools.

For example a global pharmaceutical company looking to improve plant production planning processes in one of its manufacturing locations in South America, recognised that a point solution was appropriate. In implementing a constraint based planning application it was able to drive real benefits fast.

- Reduction of the planning cycle from 13 to 5 days, thereby increasing agility.
- Significant improvement in data accuracy — bills of materials, routings, open orders.
- Redeployment of staff due to efficiency improvements.
- $700,000 reduction in annual operating costs.
- Reduced inventory levels.

This gave the company a platform on which to build and develop its quite immature supply chain.

At the other end of the spectrum a highly successful global consumer electronics company recognised that to succeed they had to ensure that the "absolute latest" — not just a recent model was on the shelf. However, they also realised that they alone could not guarantee this. For them collaboration with their customers and suppliers was essential to deliver a supply chain with zero stock.

Within the company, the demand and production planning functions were improved to provide a solid foundation before asking customers and suppliers to collaborate.

Work was then focused on customers and more closely coupling supply with their forecast and actual demand. Weekly demand pulses from nine major customers were translated into manufacturing schedules. Electronic linkages were established for forecasting and point of sale data collection from these nine, with the capability to link all the customers. Electronic commerce linkages were formed with key suppliers to streamline the flow of manufacture through to customers.

In reality, then, selecting a solution to meet one's current needs and which will work are the most important criteria.

In the case of one engineering company, which had difficulties in providing accurate delivery dates, the promise of on-line available to promise data was a great temptation. It implemented a full scale end-to-end APS system only to find that the poor reliability of its manufacturing processes rendered any date useless. For this firm a point solution to help manage their manufacturing operations was required.

This mistake was costly in terms of expenditure on systems but also delayed it from addressing the real problems which eventually undermined the potential for the whole business.

However, in another pharmaceutical company which had tried many times, without success, to improve forecasting, the implementation of a cross-functional solution provided the catalyst for making a real difference. For the first time the advanced APS forecasting software could support the process and provide the ability to aggregate demand to a global level. By removing the technical boundaries the implementation of the APS solution resulted in a radical improvement in forecast accuracy and associated areas:

- Forecast accuracy improvement of 22%.
- Reduction in finished goods inventory levels and the ability to apply statistical safety stocks.
- Redeployment of planners due to efficiency improvements (managing forecasts on an exception basis).
- Global event planning using aggregation and reconciliation.
- Global process providing clear accountability, enabled by a three tier performance metric.

In conclusion, there is no one right answer. The vendors will always try to paint a wonderful picture of what could be achieved. It is important that one makes sure one can see how this will be achieved and focus on making small gains quickly rather than big gains never.

Collaborative planning — false hope or inevitable consequence?

If collaboration is so good why isn't everyone working together in harmony? To a certain extent it has happened. Concepts such as vendor managed inventory (VMI), continuous replenishment planning (CRP), and efficient consumer response (ECR) have all required an increased level of co-operation and collaboration between parties in a supply chain.

But what is new today is that electronic commerce is creating a new form of competition, not just between organisations, but between supply chains. The winners of this competition will be those parties that can work together to provide enhanced value to the customer.

Dell and Ford are examples of this in the high technology and automotive industries. In both, the services and products offered to the consumer are a result of the complex interaction of multiple suppliers, manufacturers and logistics providers.

The front end order capture mechanism may be Web-based, and the integration to the fulfilment process becomes a real differentiator (eg available to promise, on-line product configuration/pricing options, delivery speed options). The winners of this supply chain versus supply chain competition will be the collaborators.

The road to collaborative planning

The initial hurdle is to define the common goal and to identify the benefits for all partners. Typically, pilots start small with a limited selection of products or selected partners only.

Collaborative e-planning solutions are adopted by leading organisations that understand three new factors.

- The ability of new technology, eg extranets to support much faster and more secure sharing of data across supply chains and across multiple organisations.
- The increasing importance of the Internet as a new channel, and the rise of mass customisation.
- The increasing competition between supply chains, and hence the need for technology-enabled collaboration.

How does extranet technology support collaborative e-planning?

Extranets are an Internet-based business to business network. Extranets bring business partners together over public networks. Extranets can link companies to companies, networks to networks, and even individuals to specific software or data.

Important considerations in Extranet design include connectivity, security, protocols/standards, and security. Sharing data across organisations is a key requirement of collaborative e-planning solutions.

Where in the past EDI was a standard method of transferring data in common formats, today's extranet technology allows much faster and more direct linkage between businesses.

This is particularly important in the area of supply chain planning, where the timely sharing of key information (demand plans, production plans, available inventories etc) is of major benefit to all parties in a supply chain.

According to a Forrester study carried out in 1999, half of the Fortune 1000 companies are actively using extranet applications. This should increase significantly as the scope of electronic commerce and collaboration is extended.

Case study: US snack food firm

A market leading US-based snack foods company commissioned PricewaterhouseCoopers to design more effective forecasting and materials planning processes.

The problems included frequent stock-outs of critical raw materials which in turn caused production and supply problems further down the supply chain.

Approach
Demand **side**: Manugistics DP-EE was implemented, starting with the markets where large retailers and wholesalers accounted for a high percentage of sales.

A pilot project was undertaken with the largest of these retailers, so that actual store sales were used as the basis for the forecast for that customer.

Supply side: The key suppliers for three critical raw materials were identified. A Manugistics constrained production planning module was implemented so that the constraints of both the supplier's production capacity and the snack foods company's own manufacturing capacity were considered.

This involved working close to a limited number of suppliers to provide joint visibility of the demand forecast and production plans, and to ensure that on-hand inventory, planned orders and in-transit data was shared between the interested parties.

Benefits
- The accuracy of the forecast increased by 18% in the pilot market.
- The frequency of stock-outs at the plants was reduced because the supplier was better able to respond to changes in customer demand.
- At the same time, raw material inventories were reduced by over 25%.

Collaborative Planning — a real example

The consumer goods/retail industry has produced a good example of how this collaboration can work in practice. The industry group VICS (Voluntary Inter Industry Commerce Standards) has produced a standard approach to internet collaboration, known as the collaborative planning, forecasting and replenishment (CPFR) initiative.

According to VICS, between 15% and 25% of supply chain inventories can be eliminated through adoption of CPFR best practices.

What is collaborative planning, forecasting and replenishment (CPFR)?

CPFR requires that the buyer and seller develop a single shared forecast and update it regularly based on information shared over the Internet.

It is a business-to-business workflow over the Internet, with data exchanged dynamically, designed to increase in-stock customer service and sales while cutting inventory.

There is no single CPFR business process that fits all consumer goods and retail firms, but there is a set of CPFR alternatives, which can be mixed and matched by any group of trading partners to fit their needs. These alternatives include:
- Agree on the relationships and goal for each partner.
- Create a joint business plan.
- Develop a single forecast of consumer demand.
- Identify and resolve which forecast exceptions will be highlighted.
- Develop a single order forecast.
- Identify and resolve exceptions to the order forecast.
- Generate orders based on the constrained order forecast.

HOW ARE THE APS VENDORS RESPONDING TO THE CHALLENGE OF ELECTRONIC BUSINESS?

All the leading APS vendors are developing products to provide new functionality to support the new processes and channels associated with electronic business.

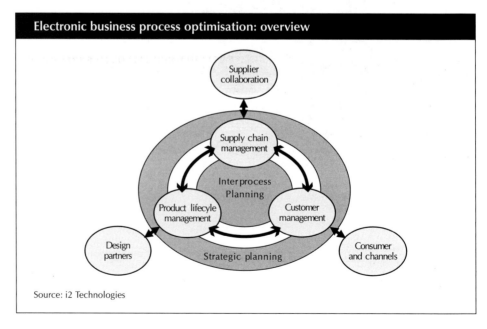

Electronic business process optimisation: overview

Source: i2 Technologies

i2 Technologies' vision of Electronic Business Process Optimisation (e-BPO) is a leading example of the likely direction these tools will take.

i2's recent acquisition of SMART Technologies is also an important marker. SMART Customer Relationship Management (CRM) applications produce Web content which helps to develop relationships with their customers and channel partners.

Manugistics is developing an e-business offering via its new NetWORKS product. The trend towards collaboration is reflected in the new functions:

- Better ATP (available to promise).
- Collaborative demand planning.
- Materials constraint planning.
- Integration with third-party logistics service providers.
- The other APS vendors are undertaking similar developments.

The combination of an APS system's ability to resolve complex supply problems and an Internet-based customer relationship tool will provide powerful functionality for tomorrow's customer-focused organisations.

ADVANCED PLANNING AND SCHEDULING — THE FUTURE

The next generation of APS will continue to build on new technologies, and will be best used by the collaborators, operating in real supply chain partnerships.

Powerful APS planning engine technologies will be at the heart of supply chain communities, providing linkage between customers and suppliers.

APS vendors will provide hosting services so that communities can access this new technology. Web front ends, increasingly used by customers for order placement, will be closely linked to a combination of integrated ERP, APS and CPM systems, ensuring that the promises made really can be fulfilled.

APS will be enhanced by the development of new features, such as exception reporting via Internet messaging, data mapping, and advanced order tracking (eg linkage to logistics systems).

KEY ISSUES FOR THE CEO
- What systems do you have, and do they have the capability to conduct business electronically?
- Are these systems able to plan your business to meet the ever changing requirements of your customers?
- How much of your whole organisation is focused to deliver what the customers want?
- Are you operating in a collaborative environment where you share information with suppliers and customers alike? Should you be?

the winning link

Everyone in the supply chain wins with leading e-procurement solutions from Commerce One.

Simplifying the process

How much time is spent obtaining essential information from product catalogues? In short, too much. The Commerce Chain Solution™ from Commerce One automates your purchasing process from requisition to order, direct from the desktop. It enables users to select products, compare prices and check availability from a multi-supplier catalogue. And everything happens in real time.

Value-add for purchasing teams

Automating the purchasing process doesn't just benefit end users. It means that you can throw away your out-of-date catalogues, relinquish lengthy administrative processes and spend more time building focused and effective supplier relationships.

Speed, efficiency, control

We can take account of your specific business rules to pre-determine spending levels for individual buyers. Preferred supplier policies are enforced to achieve volume discounts and reduce uncontrolled purchases from non-contracted suppliers.

Reduced costs – across the track

The beauty of our e-procurement solution is that it is truly end-to-end. By automating the entire goods and services supply chain we can help both buyers and suppliers achieve significantly reduced operational costs and increased efficiency.

The result: end users gain access to fast, reliable and efficient purchasing and you can focus on improving strategic supplier relationships. This is why leading buyers and their suppliers are selecting our solution. Join the team and prepare to win.

Call us on +1 925 941 6000
or email us at info@commerceone.com

or visit our website
www.commerceone.com
www.marketsite.net

COMMERCE ONE

Sourcing for support — e-procurement

INTRODUCTION

Buying non-production related (NPR) goods and services is now a very active area of procurement. Research has shown that a typical large corporation can spend over 30% of its revenues on NPR goods and services.

Spending on NPR goods — also called 'indirect', 'goods not for resale', 'non-bill of materials', or 'maintenance, repair and operations' — had until recently been overlooked by many organisations.

This was in part understandable. Most businesses underestimate their spend in this area (and so ignore it as being non-strategic).

Also, until recently, there was no effective way of managing this expenditure across the enterprise. The emergence of e-business has been another catalyst for a change in attitude. Technological advances are now offering ways to manage such expenditure effectively.

This chapter describes how e-business, or, specifically, e-procurement, is changing the world of NPR purchasing.

It discusses the challenges and consequences of e-procurement and the key elements of a justifiable business case.

It also details how to get the implementation strategy right and discusses some of the technologies already in the market place.

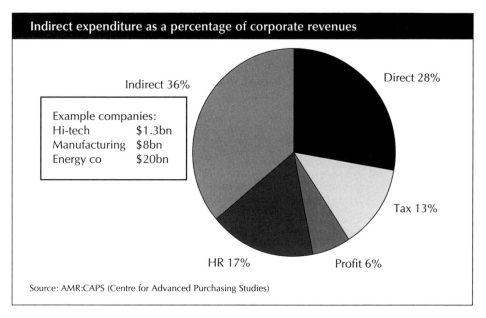

Indirect expenditure as a percentage of corporate revenues

Indirect 36%

Example companies:
Hi-tech $1.3bn
Manufacturing $8bn
Energy co $20bn

Direct 28%

Tax 13%

HR 17%   Profit 6%

Source: AMR:CAPS (Centre for Advanced Purchasing Studies)

CONTROLLING NPR PROCUREMENT

Early attempts to manage NPR procurement focused on process cost reduction. The general observation was that this area of expenditure took a disproportionate amount of resources to manage — 80% effort for 20% of value is a ratio often quoted.

Until recently, purchasing cards (P-cards) were the selected instrument of choice. They offer consolidated billing, a large reduction in paperwork and a minimum management overhead. Unfortunately, such schemes were often poorly implemented, resulting in a mushrooming of the supplier base. They also address the area of least potential benefit.

Non-production — the Cinderella of purchasing

- On average over 30% of gross revenue is spent on non-production (indirect) purchases.
- These goods and services are bought by non-production related purchasers (often part-timers), armed with paper catalogues, fax machine and the telephone, and are high-volume/low-value purchases.
- Tens of thousands of purchases are required each year to keep a company running, leaving lots of room for inefficiencies.
- The process to purchase such items often drives employees to work outside the organisation's central systems.
- Procurement staff are focusing on administrative tasks rather than negotiating improved relationships with suppliers.
- Lack of overview of purchasing volumes prevents negotiation of the best deals.
- Leveraged contracts are difficult to implement across multi-site organisations (employees often don't know of their existence).
- The transactional effort, and therefore cost for a low value item is often identical to that of a major purchase.

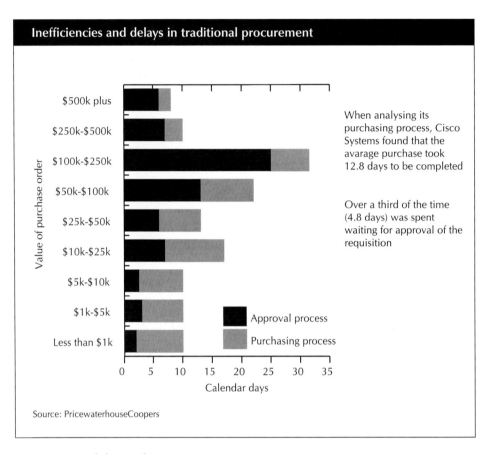

Inefficiencies and delays in traditional procurement

When analysing its purchasing process, Cisco Systems found that the avarage purchase took 12.8 days to be completed

Over a third of the time (4.8 days) was spent waiting for approval of the requisition

Source: PricewaterhouseCoopers

A new way of doing things

Managing NPR procurement is a true cross-industry problem and independent software vendors, realising the market opportunity this represents, have rushed in with their solutions.

Over the last couple of years, Internet start-ups have been slowly followed by the ERP (enterprise resource planning) vendors. Faced with declining revenues after solving the Y2K problem, ERP vendors are looking to e-business solutions, such as e-procurement, as a way to extend the life of their products.

In the development of corporate computing, it was very often the case that, after tackling the firm's financial systems, procurement was the next target because of the close coupling with accounts payable.

So how can one integrate ERP into this? Few ERP implementations were based on a sound business case that offered a reasonable return on investment. Fortunately, e-procurement of NPR can offer a substantial return on investment, allowing a possible post-justification of the ERP investment.

Because e-procurement is essentially a point solution technology — not part of a strategic enterprise-wide architecture — it can be grafted on to almost any legacy ERP/accounting system.

Indeed, the system can be allowed to stand alone with no system integration requirements. Large organisations, in particular, have realised that NPR spend can now be effectively managed using packaged technologies — for example, combining electronic catalogues with workflow distributed over corporate intranets.

What's wrong with this picture?

Your company uses the Internet for e-mail, marketing, sales, research and more.

But you still manually approve requisitions. And fax POs to your vendors. And cut checks.

Today, you can automate your entire procurement process, eliminating costs and inefficiencies, by fully leveraging the power of the Internet. End-to-end Internet procurement solutions from Intelisys can help you improve your overall financial picture by **reducing the cost of your purchasing process by as much as 30%**. For large companies, that can mean millions of dollars in annual savings.

A growing number of Global 2000 companies such as Ford Motor Company, Texas Instruments and Chase Manhattan Bank — along with their suppliers large and small — are streamlining their purchasing processes with i-procurement solutions from Intelisys.

To learn how Intelisys can help your company,
visit www.intelisys.com, e-mail info@intelisys.com or call 1-888-294-4PRO.

Intelisys

The Internet Procurement Solution™

CHALLENGES AND CONSEQUENCES

Implementation of an e-procurement system can be viewed from two different standpoints. It is either a technological means of addressing a long-standing procurement problem, or the beginning of an organisation's transformation into an e-business.

For an established large business, e-procurement of NPR is probably the simplest and lowest risk step to explore what e-business truly means. New, far-sighted businesses have identified that e-procurement of NPR is a way to avoid creating unnecessary infrastructure and large procurement departments for its rapidly growing company.

This proposition appeals directly to the chief financial officer and chief operating officer as having a solid business case and requiring no act of faith on behalf of the board of directors. Revenue based savings on NPR expenditure go straight to the bottom line and a 10% reduction in purchase costs here could easily result in a 50% increase in profit margin.

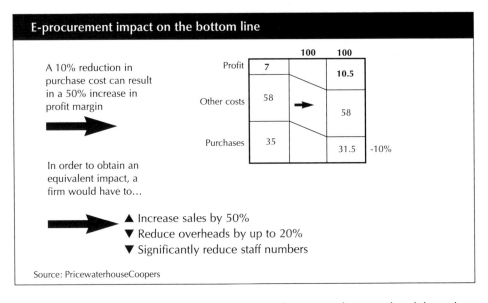

E-procurement impact on the bottom line

A 10% reduction in purchase cost can result in a 50% increase in profit margin

In order to obtain an equivalent impact, a firm would have to...

▲ Increase sales by 50%
▼ Reduce overheads by up to 20%
▼ Significantly reduce staff numbers

Source: PricewaterhouseCoopers

Whichever position is taken — procurement solution or e-business breakthrough — some crucial issues must not be overlooked.

Commodity managers

If the items on offer in the electronic catalogue have not been well negotiated, an e-procurement system will simply allow users to execute bad deals more easily. Therefore, to implement e-procurement without commodity managers and a sourcing strategy in place would be foolhardy.

The good news is, because of the quality of data from these new systems, much less work has to be done up-front in terms of spend analysis. Also, the process does not have to operate like the traditional sourcing efforts that have to be repeated every few years.

E-procurement, coupled with even low-end data warehouse technologies, offers the possibility of continuous improvement and better spend leverage than was ever possible before. Indeed, this could be the first time that the organisation will have full visibility across the company of its indirect spend.

The size of the change

The shift to e-procurement causes some important change management issues. In the procurement department, where there will be a wholesale shift from administration to supplier management, it is a large change for a small group.

For the rest of the organisation, because a large proportion of the staff will now order NPR goods and services, there will be small change for a large group. This group could number tens of thousands for a large global company and they will be asked to use a Web browser rather than a fax or telephone.

In the end, it is user behaviour that will determine the value of the e-procurement system — however good the systems might be, if they are not used then the savings are not realised.

New rules

The change within an organisation can be large, and there will need to be new processes and rules to ensure e-procurement's success.

It is PricewaterhouseCoopers' experience that, in general, the finance and administration function, along with internal audit, are more than happy to see the introduction of e-procurement. They can scrap complex business rules, which were put in place to defend paper processes and were often not followed, and they can access a complete audit trail on a purchase.

However, line management may not relish what it sees as a loss of control and potential increase in workload. Imaginative organisations are taking the view that, with post-audit capability, employees should be trusted to obey their authority limits. These companies are removing most of the checking processes. Wrong-doers can be easily identified by running periodic journal reports.

The other perceived losers are the local purchasing agents, who will fight against the loss of local contracts that may have been based on long-standing personal relationships — especially where a global or regional deal appears less good at their site.

Suppliers

In addition to the buying organisation and its people, one must also consider the impact on suppliers. For e-procurement to be a success, suppliers must agree to provide and maintain electronic feeds to a master catalogue. The software vendors have different approaches to this, but in general the ownership of catalogue management lies with the vendor, the buyer, or a third party.

Initially, it is necessary to educate suppliers so they understand what is required of them and what they may gain. Eventually, as e-procurement approaches develop but before standards are stabilised, the main challenge will be to persuade the supplier to provide the catalogue in the format the enterprise needs. This will be easier to achieve where the volume and value of purchased goods is high.

Experience from early adopters of the technology is that supplying organisations are very keen to enter such a programme with their major customers. They readily accept the benefits of increased volumes, 100% accurate purchase orders and a reduction in the sales and support staff needed to service the client. In several cases, suppliers have dramatically increased discounts and simplified pricing structures on being told that an e-procurement system was to be implemented.

Some suppliers are mistakenly building Web sites with a view to selling to corporate customers. They are missing the point. Corporations need to know what their staff members are spending their money on, and purchases on an Internet site are as bad as using the telephone or the fax — the transaction knowledge is lost. From a corporate user point of view, multiple Web sites with different looks and navigation will be unattractive compared to a standardised, and pre-approved, corporate catalogue.

THE BUSINESS CASE

In setting up the business case for board approval there are a number of important considerations. The primary one is not to depend too heavily on high-level cross-industry metrics.

A good understanding of the NPR spend and profile of the firm must be generated. Without an e-procurement system in place this will have to be done by consolidating ERP data, some sampling, and some educated guesswork.

Although the average spending on NPR might be more than 30% of revenue, it varies considerably. For a large manufacturer it could be as low as 20%, for a financial institution as high as 50%.

Additionally, the mix of goods and services will be crucial to determine the return on investment. It is relatively hard to catalogue services, although major temporary labour organisations are working towards rate cards for much of what they do.

A typical figure for 'hard' goods that can easily be bought via catalogue would be 30% of the total NPR spend. By working with suppliers of services, this can relatively easily be pushed to about 50%. Getting beyond this figure becomes increasingly difficult.

A business case will typically be based on three core areas of benefit — compliance, leverage, and process efficiency. The relative value of these to a particular organisation will depend on how much NPR work has been done before and its corporate culture in terms of control.

Compliance

This refers to the elimination of maverick buying and is typically the most important benefit area of the three.

The current level of compliance is difficult to establish but, for most enterprises, 30% to 40% would be a reasonable estimate. Organisations with e-procurement in place, such as Microsoft, claim they can reach 95% compliance with pre-negotiated contracts. The benefit of raising compliance is easily calculated by establishing the average level of discount for on-contract goods versus off-contract and multiplying by a reasonable estimate of the likely compliance with the system in place.

Leverage

Having achieved compliance with existing contracts, organisations will be able to measure true volumes of spend and be able to negotiate improved discounts or terms. The actual figure for this is usually hard to gauge before implementation, but a major client of PricewaterhouseCoopers estimates the benefit to be around 50% of the compliance savings. If done correctly, this area has even greater potential if combined with aggressive supplier management.

Process efficiency

This has been the historical focus of efforts and is as an important gain if viewed in isolation. The benefits are harder to estimate as the gains depend on the organisation structure and any previous initiatives. It may only represent 10% of compliance savings. However, this is notoriously difficult to demonstrate as much of the gain relates to a reduction in staffing but the process efficiencies often refer to the elimination of small slices of several people's jobs.

Numbers quoted from different organisations vary widely (probably due to definitional issues). A significant systems provider says it reduced the cost of processing a purchase order from around $130 to $25, and Microsoft quotes $60 down to $5. Microsoft and the others will continue to see a reducing cost per purchase order as the same number of procurement staff deal with an ever-increasing number of transactions.

Procurement transaction cycle: plan to cover the whole process

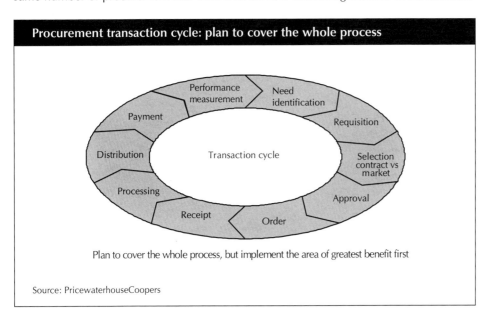

Plan to cover the whole process, but implement the area of greatest benefit first

Source: PricewaterhouseCoopers

Overall benefits

The degree and speed of potential saving is massively compelling — however it is essential to follow the analysis route detailed above to calculate business case numbers specific to one's own organisation.

The sum of the three areas of benefit will usually show a return on investment payback in well under six months of operation, even with conservative assumptions.

Having established a case at board level, and depending on corporate culture and structure, it may be necessary to work with each business unit to establish a rate of return at a their level. The use of a simple spreadsheet model containing the benefits allocated to each business unit is usually sufficient to win line management approval.

For one PricewaterhouseCoopers client, it was possible to show an internal rate of return ranging from 350% to well over 1000% at an individual site level. However, as a general principle, 'selling in' at a local level should be avoided as it can significantly delay the implementation of e-procurement across a large organisation. The preferred route is through strong corporate sponsorship of the style which is highly influential at the business unit level.

E-procurement of NPR goods and services — the principal benefits		
Compliance	**Leverage**	**Process efficiency**
Increased use of preferred suppliers	Consolidated details of actual spend with each supplier	Reduced administration burden
Reduced off-contract spending	Consolidated details of actual spend in each product category	Removal of paper processes
Reduced processing errors		*Leads to*
		Reduced error rates
	Leads to	Reduced processing time
Leads to	Full purchasing power being leveraged	Reduced fax/phone usage
More goods and services being purchased using the best commercial arrangements		Reduced on-site inventory
	Appropriate product categories targeted for preferred supplier contracts	*Enabling*
		Dedicated e-procurement staff to focus on value-added activities such as contract negotiations

IMPLEMENTATION STRATEGY

There are six key factors that will influence the implementation strategy.
- Supplier adoption and catalogue creation.
- User adoption.
- Culture adaptation and change adoption.
- Business constraints.
- Country-specific issues.
- Technical integration.

The priority of these factors needs to be decided to deliver an implementation plan that is as low risk as possible, that achieves benefits in the time-scale required, and yet enables the system to be accepted. Business and strategic objectives will influence the detail of the programme, but these factors will define the order and content of the rollout.

Of the six, the last three, although important, are specific to the implementing organisation, the tool selected and the legacy systems employed. The next part of this chapter looks at the first three factors.

Supplier adoption and catalogue creation

The completeness of on-line catalogues is critical to the success of an e-procurement system and for this supplier co-operation is essential.

Suppliers typically will have to invest in supporting the catalogue creation, and their willingness to do so will depend on the likely volume of business. By their very nature, NPR goods and services are often sourced locally and suppliers tend to be unique to a given country.

To convince national or regional suppliers to support e-procurement, the buying organisation will need to demonstrate a country-based rollout that gives suppliers a reasonable rate of return. For regional or global contracts, the catalogue contents may also need to be localised (such as for language or currency).

Resources to create, maintain and localise catalogue content will need to be costed and planned into the programme from the beginning.

There is a chicken-and-the-egg relationship between catalogue content and transaction volumes. Suppliers don't want to invest in full catalogues unless they can be sure of the transactions, and users don't want to transact electronically unless they have comprehensive catalogues to browse.

It is the eternal conflict: strategic procurement priorities versus user priorities; total spend value versus individual transactions. A solution has to be found that gets rid of low volume products but still satisfies enough users for them to use the catalogue. The rewards can be high.

A PricewaterhouseCoopers client starting with a global supplier base in the hundreds of thousands found that 50% of the NPR spend was with just 300 suppliers. Once commodities were compared this was reduced down to a mere 60 for the first catalogue — considerably reducing initial rollout costs and time-scales.

So how does one go about creating a catalogue that all parties agree with? Two competing strategies have been identified: a contract-only catalogue and a contract catalogue plus third party. There are time-scale implications for each that need to be investigated and will be specific to every organisation. One critical input to the decision is an understanding of what drives the off-contract purchases, for example ignorance of the contract, inconvenience of the contract, or unavailability of the product under the contract.

Contract-only catalogue
Here, users are only offered contracted items in the catalogue. For non-catalogue items, they make a request to a strategic sourcing team that sources new items as required and expands the catalogue as needed.

Clearly, if there is a high proportion of items for which there is no obvious contracted equivalent this could present an unmanageable workload. Getting the balance right between the two is important. Early teething problems in implementation can damage confidence in e-procurement irretrievably.

Contract catalogue plus third party
This approach provides user access to contract items and, through the use of approved third-party catalogues, other products. In this model, user spend is analysed periodically and, depending on the reason for selecting non-contract items, users are either steered towards contract items or the non-contract items are sourced into the buyer's catalogue.

A mixed approach
Blue chip companies should adopt a mixed approach, similar to the second option above, on the grounds of cost and diminishing returns. For a buying organisation to maintain its own catalogue of all items is a costly endeavour — estimated at $1 to $4

per line item a year. The contract catalogue might typically cover the small number of suppliers that make up, say, 80% of the volume. The balance of the catalogue is made up from third-party managed catalogues, which reduces overheads at the expense of some loss of control.

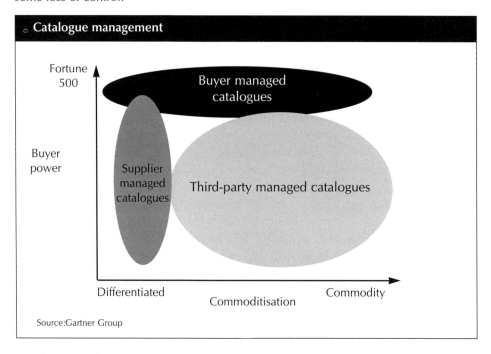

Catalogue management

Source:Gartner Group

The principle is that it is better to allow some leakage than to forfeit adoption because users are not able to find what they need. Clearly, for this to work, constant monitoring of spending patterns is required.

Creating a catalogue needs investment, both from the buyers and the suppliers. It makes sense to rationalise suppliers and reduce the number of line items before the catalogue is implemented. When this occurs, it should also be established which suppliers are willing to trade electronically for higher volumes at a lower margin.

Suppliers will quickly understand that e-procurement tilts the balance of negotiating power towards the buying organisation. E-procurement is great news in terms of increased sales if you are a preferred supplier, but the ability to maintain a preferred supplier status will mean a constant squeezing on margins as negotiated prices reflect the true buying power of the customer organisation.

After all, suppliers can be switched off and replaced in the catalogue with a mere click of a mouse.

User adoption

The biggest threat to e-procurement is the continued use of telephones, faxes and misused P-cards. One company deployed a procurement system where usage has never exceeded 5% — a disaster in terms of the e-procurement objectives.

Users must be able to order what they need easily from the system. Experience shows that users, with a choice, will rapidly abandon the new system if it takes too long to use or does not allow them to find what they need. A solution that allows off-contract requisitioning, for later judicious consolidation into the catalogue, might find early favour among an initially sceptical user community.

System usability and speed of response are critical to the acceptability of the system to the user. As an example, Mastercard knew that unless people were thrilled with the new e-procurement system, they wouldn't use it, and the project would fail. Accordingly, it trained people in smaller groups and spent a lot of time with individuals. The firm thought this area was so important that it doubled the amount of time allocated to it in the rollout plan.

For e-procurement to work, new technology and supporting processes need to be introduced to attract users in a dramatic way, changing the behaviour of the buying community to achieve a critical business goal. As an example of success, Microsoft says it has a level of 99% use of its in-house procurement system for maintenance, repair and operations items.

Reinforcing the required behaviour will usually require scrapping any paper processes and an instruction to suppliers that goods shipped without a purchase order will not be paid for — the latter of these having the most assured outcome.

Culture adaptation and change adoption

The introduction of an e-procurement system affects the whole organisation, not just the procurement function.

Although the risk and cost control benefits will drive a central, standardised solution, it is likely that variations will be necessary on a geographic or business unit basis. It is vital to develop communication and training plans aimed at reducing resistance to the change and, ideally, stimulating a positive demand for e-procurement.

During pilot trials, users' feedback can help determine how a particular e-procurement tool can be used in other situations. Using this feedback will also increase 'buy-in' but puts a heavy onus on the selection process for the representative users. The creation of 'change champions' can be the key to a successful roll-out both in terms of project resource economics and enthusiastic user adoption. This 'train the trainers' approach can significantly reduce the cost and time-scale of the global roll-out and should be mirrored in the approach to creating local technical support.

There will also be unavoidable cultural changes inherent in any e-procurement implementation. These could include the following.

- Central control of contracts, catalogues and price updates.
- Maintenance of explicit business rules.
- Increased usage of alliance suppliers.
- Reduction/elimination of user choice of vendor.
- Potential overturning of long-established local supply agreements and relationships.
- A switch from traditional communication (phone/fax) to PC-based ordering.
- Greater IT literacy requirements for users and procurement staff.
- Increased rigour in the authorisation processes.
- Changes to goods-in/goods-received practices.
- Greater visibility of individual and unit spending patterns.
- Accountability for the use of the system.
- Realignment of roles and responsibilities.
- Change in the work balance of procurement support staff, from administration to strategic sourcing.
- Headcount reductions as part of the economic return on the project.

SOFTWARE SOLUTIONS

Many software application vendors have developed solutions for e-procurement. The table below lists some common examples. The best solution for a particular buying organisation will depend on issues such as the organisation's technical infrastructure, its preferred approach to catalogue management and whether it has any requirement for multiple language and multiple currency facilities.

Common software solutions for e-procurement		
Supplier	**Product**	**Website**
Commerce One	Market site/BuySite	www.commerceone.com
Harbinger	Trusted Link Catalog	www.harbinger.com
BAAN	E-procurement	www.baan.com
American Tech	PurchasingNet	www.purchasingnet.com
Ariba	ORMS	www.ariba.com
Agentics	SupplyChannel	www.agentics.com
Fisher Technology	ProcureNet	www.procurenet.com
Sun/Netscape	BuyerExpert	www.netscape.com
SAP	SAP BBP	www.sap.com/products/bbp
Oracle	Internet procurement	www.oracle.com

Selection of the procurement technology would normally run in parallel with, or slightly ahead of, the development of the business case. This is necessary as there is a big variation in the licensing models and pricing used by the vendors, as well as some differences in the stated benefits of each package.

Once the vendor has been selected, the right cost model can be incorporated into the business case. Some companies take the view that, because of the potentially huge rate of return, the absolute price of the software application is not the issue — rather the risks associated with successful implementation and speed of implementation should be given priority in the assessment.

The outsourcing alternative

An alternative to developing a corporate owned and operated solution is the outsourcing of the procurement function to a third party that manages the electronic catalogues and also the supplier relationship on behalf of multiple buyers.

There are various business models for such an arrangement. Potentially the most attractive is one that leverages spend across a number of buying organisations and so achieves a better price than would be possible for any one of the buyers on their own.

Such an arrangement may take the form of a purchasing consortium instead of being fully outsourced.

E-procurement provided on this basis offers a number of benefits.

- Buyers win through efficiency gains, better control of expenditure and greater leverage of supplier relationships. A hosted e-procurement service can also make these gains available to small and medium businesses, in addition to larger corporate customers.
- Suppliers win through efficiency gains, plus access to a larger population of customers.

- Hosting organisations win through building communities, strengthening relationships with customers (if operated by a supplier of other services) and through leveraging their data warehouses to provide procurement best practice services.
- Rapid implementation is possible, although the change management challenges in the buying organisation remain.

Several organisations are now starting to offer e-procurement services on an outsourced basis — including PricewaterhouseCoopers itself.

Looking forward

Over the next one to three years the majority of the Global 500 organisations will initiate e-procurement programmes.

The way will be led by the largest of these. They have the largest potential return on investment, based on the volume of spend that they will bring under management. As the risks and rewards of such implementations become better understood, and the supplier base becomes acclimatised to this new way of buying, so e-procurement will cascade down through the business world.

For small and medium businesses, the cost of acquisition and maintenance of such systems will remain a barrier until there is general availability of managed catalogues, such as that from BT/ CommerceOne.

The spread of managed catalogues and associated outsourced procurement services will be greatly facilitated by the introduction of the XML mark-up language. This allows the exchange of commercial information between different procurement buy-side applications and third-party operated catalogue or transaction services. XML is also the answer for configurable products (such as PCs) and variable priced services (such as printing and temporary labour) — in future, a calculation engine built by the supplier into its own Web page can be linked back to the buyer's e-procurement tool.

Over time, larger enterprises that had chosen to develop an in-house system will move to the outsource model. This will be achieved by either spinning out their procurement organisation as a new business — offering a shared service for themselves and third parties — or buying-in the procurement function from an established organisation.

E-procurement is in the first wave of business-to-business electronic commerce. It has a value proposition second to none and will be the start for many organisations' move towards an e-business model. Implementing e-procurement, while relatively low risk, is not risk free and, in particular, change management and stakeholder management must be well executed.

KEY ISSUES FOR THE CEO

- What proportion of your cost base is non-production related goods and services?
- How is it currently managed?
- What benefits will e-procurement bring to your business?
- What items would most benefit from e-procurement solution?
- What cultural changes do you need to engender to make e-procurement implementation a success?
- Is the outsourcing of the procurement of goods and services an option for your business?

Our customers won't **reveal** how they're **saving** **$2 billion.**

▶ And no wonder.

Aspect is the competitive advantage customers won't talk about. More than 150 of the world's largest companies are saving billions of dollars with Aspect's solutions for Inbound Supply Chain Management. Aspect's Web-based *eDesign*™, *eSource*™ and *eOperate*™ give customers the competitive edge by optimizing product development, sourcing and operations. **Example? IBM: $250 million straight to the bottom line.**

Want to improve *your* bottom line?
Contact Aspect at **1-800-734-7279** or **www.aspectdv.com**
to order your free Aspect ROI video.

aspect
DEVELOPMENT
Global Leader in Inbound Supply Chain Management

Sourcing for production — e-design

INTRODUCTION

The previous chapter showed how e-business, specifically, e-procurement, is changing the world of non-production related (or indirect) goods and services. The benefits from the application of e-procurement to indirect purchases are clear:

- Compliance to well negotiated contracts with preferred suppliers.
- Leverage from consolidating organisation-wide purchases.
- Improved purchasing processes in an area of high volume, low value transactions.

But what of e-business in the context of direct purchases?

For direct materials, new e-business technology is creating opportunities for companies to increase shareholder value through the integration of their inbound supply chain management with strategic sourcing and strategic product development.

This chapter predicts that there will be a revolution in the inbound supply chain process in the near future. In addition to executives becoming far more aware of the value that best practice procurement can add to an organisation, there will be a proliferation of advanced planning tools available in an area of the supply chain to help realise this potential.

The revolution will be driven by developments in supporting e-business technology that will enable procurement to make significant contributions to bottom line profitability. This technology will ensure the delivery of benefits in both direct and indirect goods and services.

This chapter shows that electronic catalogues and electronic workflow will be combined with on-line systems that allow the integration of sourcing and product development strategies across procurement, design and manufacturing regardless of location. As over two-thirds of direct material costs can be built in during design and development, this will offer significant opportunities for progressive companies.

The speed and level of return show that this will be an area of significant investment by progressive companies in the short to medium term. By undertaking this planned investment and re-engineering of the associated processes, firms will soon be using the inbound supply chain as a means of achieving competitive advantage and not simply a supporting process to reduce cost.

CREATING COMPETITIVE ADVANTAGE THROUGH E-BUSINESS

E-business will create added value for the enterprise by expediting and integrating sourcing and product development strategies through:

- Centralised repositories of information for parts, services, suppliers and commodities that can easily be shared and transferred across the organisation.
- Speeding communications between suppliers and buyers throughout both organisations. It provides direct supplier updates and pre-release product information that is stored in real time between the two parties.
- Automated fulfilment between buyers and suppliers, with on-line tracking of goods and services.
- Collaborative design between suppliers and manufacturers.
- Optimising new designs to meet time-to-market and cost objectives.

MAXIMISING VALUE DURING NEW PRODUCT DEVELOPMENT

It is common for over 70% of the cost of direct materials to be fixed at the development stage. It is then impractical and costly to influence these costs for the remainder of a product's life, leaving procurement (often excluded from the design phase) only able to influence the remaining 30% of costs.

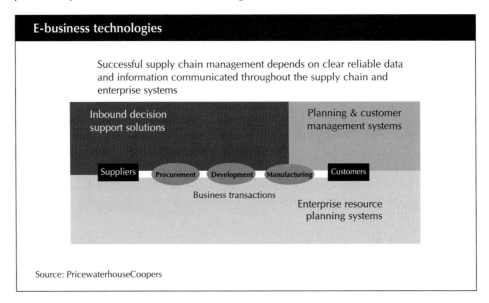

E-business technologies

Successful supply chain management depends on clear reliable data and information communicated throughout the supply chain and enterprise systems

Inbound decision support solutions

Planning & customer management systems

Suppliers | Procurement | Development | Manufacturing | Customers

Business transactions

Enterprise resource planning systems

Source: PricewaterhouseCoopers

To address this, new e-business technology offers a highly effective way to deliver dramatic business benefits by acting as a bridge for information flows between the design, sourcing and supply chain teams during new product development.

The impact on the business can be significant. Revenue enhancement and cost reduction, through integrated product development and procurement, can be related to the core drivers of value, allowing the impact on shareholder value to be directly gauged.

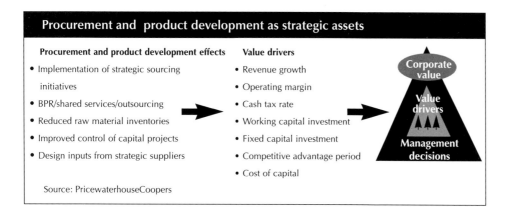

Procurement and product development as strategic assets

Procurement and product development effects

- Implementation of strategic sourcing initiatives
- BPR/shared services/outsourcing
- Reduced raw material inventories
- Improved control of capital projects
- Design inputs from strategic suppliers

Value drivers

- Revenue growth
- Operating margin
- Cash tax rate
- Working capital investment
- Fixed capital investment
- Competitive advantage period
- Cost of capital

Corporate value

Value drivers

Management decisions

Source: PricewaterhouseCoopers

BARRIERS THAT REDUCE EFFECTIVENESS

There are several barriers that reduce the effectiveness of the typical inbound supply chain.

Management of purchased goods and services tends to be fragmented. Typically, engineering and design teams dictate sourcing strategies without the full involvement of the procurement or sourcing unit. Procurement teams often have a narrow and functional view of the total product development process, resulting in lost opportunities to create value.

There are often too many suppliers servicing a specific commodity. In some cases companies have multiple agreements with the same supplier but with differing terms.

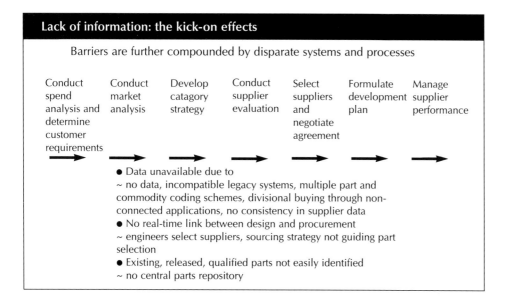

Lack of information: the kick-on effects

Barriers are further compounded by disparate systems and processes

Conduct spend analysis and determine customer requirements → Conduct market analysis → Develop catagory strategy → Conduct supplier evaluation → Select suppliers and negotiate agreement → Formulate development plan → Manage supplier performance

- Data unavailable due to
  ~ no data, incompatible legacy systems, multiple part and commodity coding schemes, divisional buying through non-connected applications, no consistency in supplier data
- No real-time link between design and procurement
  ~ engineers select suppliers, sourcing strategy not guiding part selection
- Existing, released, qualified parts not easily identified
  ~ no central parts repository

As a consequence, the supplier profile for many corporations is highly fragmented, making any type of strategic supplier management or partnering difficult.

Procurement teams often lack the corporate-wide view. This lack of view of supplier performance across different product and commodity areas (especially where legacy systems exist), makes strategic sourcing difficult.

Design teams often lack vital commercial information. This would enable them to make optimal sourcing decisions for new products.

MAKING PRODUCT DEVELOPMENT MORE EFFECTIVE

The return from optimising these processes and reducing complexity can be calculated in tens of millions of dollars and there is a strong trend to measure this area more effectively. Key trends can be categorised as follows.

Greater internal integration between design, manufacturing and the rest of the enterprise. This has been an ambition for many companies for many years but most lack the organisation, performance management processes and technology to allow it.

Greater integration with suppliers. And so linking external and internal supply chain processes.

Rationalisation of suppliers and the development of strategic partners. Companies will develop closer relationships with fewer, but better, suppliers to meet their needs. In some cases, they will operate shared objectives and targets in the areas of product design and order fulfilment, with contracts replaced by partnership agreements.

Increased flexibility and agility. This will be critical as technology and product life cycles shorten in the future.

Leverage over commodities and services globally and regionally. Companies will develop sourcing strategies that aggregate demand globally or regionally, to benefit from increased economies of scale from suppliers. To achieve this, there needs to be transparency of real-time data and information to support the sourcing decision.

The availability of decision support tools in the inbound supply chain. Buyers and designers will have a number of workbenches to support the sourcing processes providing all of the necessary information to develop sourcing strategies.

USING TECHNOLOGY TO CREATE COMPETITIVE ADVANTAGE

To exploit these opportunities, there will be significant investments in enabling technologies and processes. This will change the way direct goods and materials are sourced.

Harnessing inbound supply chain data

This will become a fundamental resource of the business. At the moment, in many businesses, this data is difficult to access. This could be because of an absence of shared internal databases, or different systems being used in different countries or product divisions, which, in turn, are different again from suppliers. This should change as investments in enabling technologies grow.

Improvements in decision support tools for strategic sourcing

There is an increasing trend to take only the purchasing decision that is optimal for the overall performance of the business. Recognising that many organisations do not rely on the lowest price as the sole selection criterion, there is a need for robust, objective decision support tools and systems to manage processes such as make-or-buy, supplier selection/evaluation and component selection.

Collaborative forecasting, planning and replenishment systems

If one works in partnership with suppliers, then one must also help manage their capacity in an integrated fashion. If this is performed successfully then the supplier can be treated as an extension to the supply chain, with mutual benefits for both parties.

Web-enabled communication with supply chain partners

There will be a vast increase in the use of e-business and Internet applications, used both internally and externally to jointly manage the supply chain.

Procurement organisation flexibility

There will be a revolution in procurement for companies that have made this investment. They will have the ability to control and influence a far greater percentage of their external expenditure using a variety of organisation models. The model best suited to their needs will be supported by a single, transparent supply chain workbench which will enable component sourcing to be co-ordinated and executed across new boundaries. The days of the centralised versus decentralised procurement organisation debate will become a thing of the past.

THE IMPACT OF E-BUSINESS

E–business solutions will create central, common, unified repositories of information that will be transparent across the enterprise. They will contain commercial and technical data on raw materials, components and suppliers. The solutions will integrate internal information across the various legacy databases and bills of materials with supplier information.

E-business solutions will provide decision support tools that enable users to search, compare, analyse, select and re-use components. This will in turn provide a strong platform to allow companies to move to the best practice scenario in inbound supply chain and direct materials procurement.

Through e-business solutions, companies will be able to build up a single database of all the parts purchased with a single company reference number. This database of common parts will encourage the re-use of components across different divisions, products and geographies.

Designers will aim to use parts that are already used, and purchasers in other divisions and locations will re-use common components from across the organisation.

The result is faster new product introduction and cheaper products.

These e-business tools can quickly become the essential building blocks for best practice sourcing strategies, strategic design decision-making and the development of preferred component and supplier programmes.

Benefits from the e-procurement of direct materials relate to the total and rapid streamlining of the inbound supply chain. They can be categorised into four key areas:

commodity leverage, supplier rationalisation, materials management consolidation and strategic product development (that is, 'design for buy').

Commodity leverage
Savings of between 5% to 11% are possible in inbound component costs. By having the ability to aggregate spend across the whole of the organisation, irrespective of how many databases are used to hold the current information, it provides the sourcing teams with on-line, up-to-date information and tools to analyse spend and sourcing options rapidly, irrespective of organisational boundaries and location.

Supplier rationalisation
Savings of between 4% to 9% are possible in component costs and through reducing the cost of administration.

By having fewer but better suppliers, supplier management and performance measurement can be undertaken to monitor the levels of service provided to the organisation and also minimising any risks in the supply chain. Having fewer suppliers also provides further opportunities to consolidate volumes of commodities to a smaller supply base.

Materials management consolidation
Savings of between 5% to 7% are possible through the reduction in inventory holding costs. A reduction in the number of new components required in the design process can provide an inventory reduction opportunity, in terms of value and stock holding space, within the warehouses.

It can eliminate existing duplicate part numbers and reduce the administration around introducing new components for a new design.

Strategic product development
Savings of 10%+ are possible in component costs and through reducing the costs and time-to-market of the new product design process.

By using all, or a combination of, the above, there is the added opportunity to benefit from designing manufacturability into as many of the new designs as possible. By optimising the best components selection process and reducing the number of additions and deletions to the preferred components database required for a new design, there is additional benefit to be gained throughout the total supply chain. The time to market for new products can also be improved, with some companies having achieved over 30% reduction in time to launch.

Optimal performance

Investments in e-business technology will enable the optimal performance of this area of new product development in the supply chain.

The following diagram reflects how best practice organisations will manage their inbound supply chain.

Buyers of the future will be far more aware of product design issues and constraints. In turn, design engineers will become commercially focused — both via the transparency of common data between the two departments and by the use of the advanced decision support tools provided by the implementation of e-business enabling technologies.

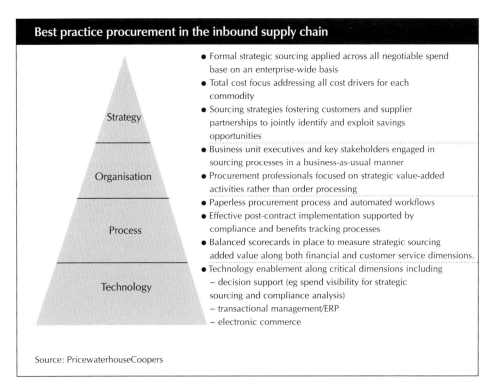

Best practice procurement in the inbound supply chain

Strategy
- Formal strategic sourcing applied across all negotiable spend base on an enterprise-wide basis
- Total cost focus addressing all cost drivers for each commodity
- Sourcing strategies fostering customers and supplier partnerships to jointly identify and exploit savings opportunities

Organisation
- Business unit executives and key stakeholders engaged in sourcing processes in a business-as-usual manner
- Procurement professionals focused on strategic value-added activities rather than order processing

Process
- Paperless procurement process and automated workflows
- Effective post-contract implementation supported by compliance and benefits tracking processes
- Balanced scorecards in place to measure strategic sourcing added value along both financial and customer service dimensions.

Technology
- Technology enablement along critical dimensions including
  ~ decision support (eg spend visibility for strategic sourcing and compliance analysis)
  ~ transactional management/ERP
  ~ electronic commerce

Source: PricewaterhouseCoopers

This will allow costs to be squeezed at the beginning of the supply chain and will also enable sustainable advantage through strategic product development.

SO HOW CAN E-PROCUREMENT DO IT?

Typical e-business solutions and tools in this area can be grouped into the following two themes: strategic sourcing and strategic product development.

Strategic sourcing

Current situation in a procurement department
Sourcing agents do not have a total view on expenditure, stock levels and forecasting data across the whole of the organisation, and have to use many separate systems to access this information. They do not have the ability to control and influence the spend across commodity groupings. The procurement teams are divorced from the decision-making points within the product development process and have a narrow view of the total inbound supply chain process.

Enabling technology to address this issue
- Web-enabled, data catalogues with cross-referencing capabilities for multiple part numbering schemes.
- Commodity management support tools — for enterprise-wide commodity leverage analysis, supplier rationalisation, materials consolidation.
- Procurement decision support tools — for supplier performance, compliance monitoring, procurement benefits tracking — all at the desktop, Web enabled.
- On-line ability to communicate sourcing strategies with design engineers, manufacturing operations and buying teams.

Strategic product development

Current situation in a design team

Design engineers cannot find essential component data with the associated commercial influence and the available data is out-of-date and held on multiple databases. It is difficult for the relevant departments (for example, procurement and manufacturing operations) to contribute to the design discussion and decisions on component selection. Design decisions are being made in isolation from the rest of the organisation and with little commercial awareness and influence.

Enabling technology to address issues

- Web-enabled component information databases available to all interested parties, on-line and with up to date information.
- On-line preferred supplier databases with access by key decision personnel.
- Total cost of ownership and lifecycle-costing models and tools, on-line for faster decision-making capability in component selection, also assisting any make versus buy decision within the manufacturing process.

A summary of the possible architecture landscape in this area can be demonstrated in the following diagram.

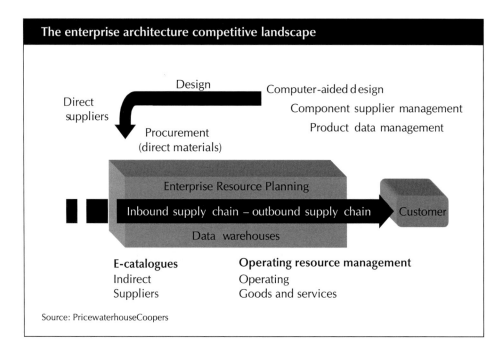

The enterprise architecture competitive landscape

Source: PricewaterhouseCoopers

This shows how the enabling technologies are rapidly and constantly being developed to respond to all of these issues, challenges and opportunities.

New suppliers are using the ERP backbone as a platform for new advanced planning and decision support tools within the inbound supply chain. In addition to these new suppliers, the ERP vendors have aspirations to extend their offerings and functionality over the next few years.

New alliances and partnerships are regularly being formed between suppliers and the competitive landscape looks very dynamic over the short to medium term.

AVAILABLE TECHNOLOGIES

One of the foremost total solutions in inbound supplier management is Aspect Development's component supplier management (CSM) solutions suite. This is designed to reduce product cost, operations expenses and design cycle time by providing strategic decision support tools for all members of cross-functional sourcing teams, including procurement, product development and manufacturing.

Here is a summary of Aspect Development's solution set:

CSM catalogue management. A set of enterprise-wide component and supplier catalogues based on current, complete and correct information organised in a standard classification scheme for ease of search, comparison, analysis, re-use and optimisation.

Preferred component and supplier management. A set of decision support tools for the sourcing teams to use when managing preferred parts and suppliers.

Life cycle management. A set of tools and databases to assist organisations to manage components throughout their lifecycle ie analysis and process management.

Strategic design management. This enables engineers to quickly find and re-use existing designs and to analyse these quickly to create new products, utilising on-line data-marts.

Strategic sourcing management. A set of decision support tools available at the sourcing agents desktop to link with the CSM catalogues to enable optimal buying power leverage within the corporation ie consolidating all components and commodity purchases across all business units with preferred suppliers, again via strategic data-marts.

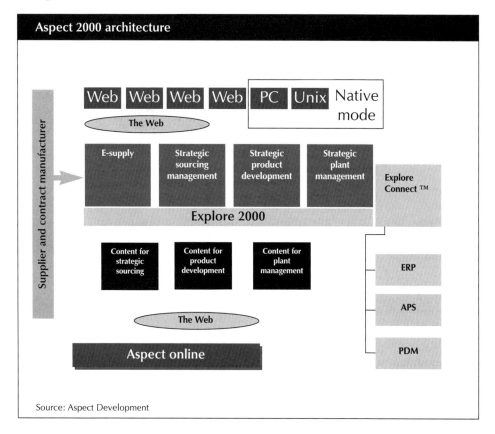

Source: Aspect Development

Solution providers are rapidly developing their capability as a content provider for internal and external catalogues in the inbound supply chain. This should be a major growth area in the future. Content management will comprise engineering, sourcing and operations data.

Both the internal and external feeds to the catalogue will be automatic and on-line to the sourcing decision points.

The chart below shows part of Aspect Development's product range and how it fits together.

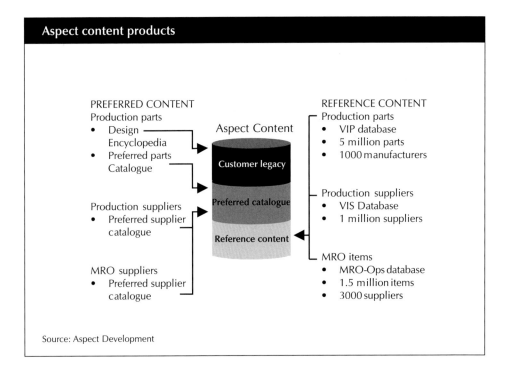

Aspect content products

PREFERRED CONTENT
Production parts
- Design — Encyclopedia
- Preferred parts Catalogue

Production suppliers
- Preferred supplier catalogue

MRO suppliers
- Preferred supplier catalogue

Aspect Content

Customer legacy

Preferred catalogue

Reference content

REFERENCE CONTENT
Production parts
- VIP database
- 5 million parts
- 1000 manufacturers

Production suppliers
- VIS Database
- 1 million suppliers

MRO items
- MRO-Ops database
- 1.5 million items
- 3000 suppliers

Source: Aspect Development

Aspect provides 'Reference Content' and 'Preferred Content' for every facet of the inbound supply chain. This covers items and suppliers of direct materials and specialised indirect maintenance, repair and operations (MRO) supplies.

The 'VIP Database' is a technical database of electronic and electro-mechanical components. It covers 1,000 manufacturers and five million parts. It delivers current and complete information for part search, analysis, selection and re-use. This enables engineers to optimise their designs and slashes design cycle time.

The 'MRO Ops Database' is a database of specialised MRO operational supplies typically used for plant maintenance and operations. The database includes electrical apparatus and equipment, wiring supplies, electronic parts, construction materials, hardware and tools, plumbing equipment, industrial equipment, machinery and supplies.

The 'VIS Database' provides users with a central repository of supplier information to support supplier sourcing processes, commodity management and supplier rationalisation. Suppliers are cross-referenced to the commodities they provide. The database contains sourcing and demographic data on suppliers, which are selected by the customer according to the commodities and regions required. It can support global sourcing strategies.

The 'Preferred Parts Catalogue' is a custom reference database targeted at customer-specified preferred components and manufacturers. Its purpose is to provide complete technical reference data for all customer-preferred components. It extends the breadth of Aspect's VIP Reference Database to provide 100% coverage of the commercial parts required by a customer to support material searching, comparison, supplier source identification, material consolidation, supplier rationalisation, alternate part identification and other CSM functions.

KEY ISSUES FOR THE CEO

- What proportion of your cost base is direct materials?
- How much of this is fixed at the development stage?
- How can you include e-procurement solutions in your key purchase strategies?
- What tools do you have to support the procurement of direct materials?
- What systems links does your business have with its supply base?
- What commercial information is provided to your design teams?
- Do the procurement teams get involved in product development through its whole cycle?
- What effect would reduced product costs, accelerated time-to-market and improved quality have on performance and shareholder value?
- What impact could e-procurement have on your organisation's profitability?

E-essentials — the technology that drives the change

INTRODUCTION

The role of technology as an enabler of e-business is a recurring theme of this book. But what is it about the technology that makes e-business feasible? This chapter introduces some of the core technology components that make it all work. The subject is huge and changing rapidly.

After describing a basic Web architecture, the chapter discusses the main hardware and software standards that make e-business work. It then moves on to how the Web is used, describing such concepts as e-catalogues, configurators and commerce platforms. Because of this book's emphasis on supply chain management, a section has been included on the importance of integration with a business's enterprise systems. Such systems are the backbone of end-to-end supply chain efficiency. The final section deals with the techniques that improve usability and, importantly, trust between users.

Much of the information in this chapter has been sourced from the PricewaterhouseCoopers' publication E-business Technology Forecast issued by the firm's technology centre in Menlo park, California (www.pwc-tech-forecast.com).

FOUR STEPS TO E-TRADING FULFILMENT

Most organisations go through a series of evolutionary steps in transacting business on the Internet.

First, they establish a Web presence that represents the company. Often called "electronic brochure-ware," this presence describes the company's basic products, services, and contact information. All major companies have reached this first step because it is simple to create and maintain a read-only file for interested parties.

The second major step is to enable a business to function through the Web, such as by allowing customers to place orders and track their status using Web browsers. Business partners can tap into a company's information systems using extranets. These business functions are an alternate channel for conducting business, but the Web is not the sole method of doing so.

This step is crucial because customers and partners are performing read/write operations with company databases, and this makes issues of data integrity, security, recovery, and system availability highly important.

Once a company achieves substantial experience on the Web, it is ready for the third major step: tying a business function to the Web as the primary mechanism for conducting its daily business. For example, one market sector that is increasingly shifting to the Web is software sales. Many software vendors are refocusing their business models from physical stores, where shelf space is very competitive, to distribution via downloads from Web sites.

The final step in e-business is to have most mission-critical applications completely available via the Web without an alternate means to conduct business. Most major industries that use electronic data interchange (EDI) require their partners to conduct business electronically, as is the case in auto manufacturing and banking.

Companies in these industries connect most of their major business processes via workflow applications with their partners through all stages of product fulfilment. All partners must design their systems so there is no single point of failure and fast recovery is always available.

In addition to this type of inter-company communication, each enterprise will use e-business technologies to integrate disparate business functions on different platforms using a common backbone.

BASIC ARCHITECTURE

Web computing provides the platform for a new style of application architecture and deployment. Web-based e-business systems consist of numerous components operating in a reliable and secure manner. The figure below illustrates how a simple e-business site might be assembled. The primary element is a Web server, which runs a program that implements the HyperText Transfer Protocol (HTTP) to exchange messages between the server and a Web browser. The server typically hosts the seller's Web home page, catalogue and order methods.

Another element often includes a payment gateway or an external service to validate and authorise credit card transactions or other payment methods.

A third element may be integration between the Web storefront and back-office systems and applications allowing traditional retailers and catalogue merchants to leverage their existing systems and infrastructure.

As e-business sites have become more functionally complex and feature-rich, and as traffic to these sites has increased, the simple Web server architecture has expanded rapidly into tiers of application and database servers. This expanded architecture allows high-performance e-business sites to achieve greater scalability and flexibility.

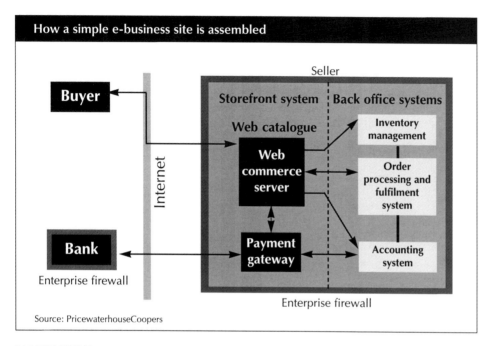

How a simple e-business site is assembled

Source: PricewaterhouseCoopers

HARDWARE

As Internet architecture has become more and more advanced, so the hardware components on both the server and client sides have increased in range and sophistication.

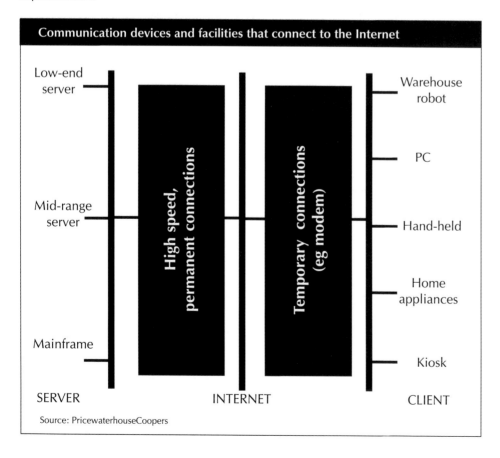

Communication devices and facilities that connect to the Internet

Source: PricewaterhouseCoopers

The previous figure illustrates the range of communication facilities and devices that connect to the Internet and the kinds of clients and servers connected to the Internet today.

Critically, the range of devices is expanding to include Internet-enabled home appliances and make the technology pervasive in consumers' lives. This will allow a deeper understanding of consumer behaviour and will create a shift in ownership — from the channel owner selling shelf space to gain consumer attention to the consumer selling their information.

One key feature of Internet Protocol (IP) based networks is that any computer system that implements the IP suite can connect to the network. By running the appropriate software, such a system can then function as a server, as a client, or as both.

SOFTWARE STANDARDS AND LANGUAGES

The ability to connect hardware components to the Internet only yields benefits when combined with standardised software tools.

This section looks briefly at some of the software standards and languages that ensure that web users all get the same message.

HTML (HyperText Markup Language)

The HTTP protocol defines the messages that can be exchanged between a Web server and a Web client.

HTML is a document description language that consists of text and fixed tags. Tags describe the attributes of the text and other content and are used by clients to determine how to display the text or perform other manipulations. Each version of HTML has added new tags, which then must be implemented by all clients. A tag is enclosed in "<" and ">" symbols, such as <B> where the text that follows the tag must be bold.

XML (eXtensible Markup Language)

XML is a more sophisticated and flexible language which allows data to be manipulated in more intelligent ways.

Intranets, extranets and the Internet — some definitions

The benefits of software standards such as HTML and XML go beyond their use on the public Internet.

Within an organisation, individual pieces of hardware are normally connected to each other by a hard-wired network, which cannot be accessed from outside. They may still, however, benefit from sharing information in the HTML or XML formats designed for the Internet. This application of information sharing on an internal, private network is referred to as an intranet.

To communicate securely with business partners, an organisation will commonly use the infrastructure of the Internet, but reserve channels that are not available to the general public. This controlled access to information creates an extranet.

XML and HTML were both developed as subsets of the Standard Generalised Markup Language (SGML), but, unlike HTML, which is a fixed language, XML can generate new special-purpose languages for specific applications.

XML is not a replacement for HTML. HTML is a specific presentation or formatting language for content on the Web. XML is a specification for generating new languages.

Electronic data interchange and XML

Traditional EDI (electronic data interchange) systems require a network connection between the two organisations that are exchanging documents. It needs a dedicated line running between the two companies.

However, the advent of the Internet has created a common communications platform upon which business can be conducted.

The universal connectivity provided by the Internet allows multitudes of additional parties, particularly small and mid-sized businesses and consumers, to use EDI technology at a lower cost. In addition, Internet-based EDI reduces transaction cycle time by using direct transfer instead of mailboxes.

Using an XML-based language for EDI overcomes many of the problems of traditional protocol-based approaches. In particular, this procedure allows more flexibility in defining new formats.

Programming and scripting languages

Various development languages are used for writing e-business platform applications. Although some languages have historically been "client" or "server" languages, the trend is to find the same languages used in both environments.

The three most common script or interpreted languages for the Internet are Java, Java-Script, and VBScript, which resembles Visual Basic.

Languages are designed to be platform-independent and can be processed by a Web browser running on any client operating system as long as the browser understands that language.

CATALOGUES, CONFIGURATORS AND COMMERCE PLATFORMS

Now that the importance of both integrated hardware and standardised software languages for the Web has been established, it is worth looking at the application software that businesses use to present their market propositions. These can loosely be grouped as catalogues, configurators and combined tools such as commerce platforms.

On-line catalogues provide a mechanism for sellers to present their products to potential buyers. Configurator software guides customers to define a product that meets given criteria and whose features and options are mutually compatible.

Once items have been selected or products configured, the purchase transaction needs to be concluded: selections verified, prices extended, orders totalled, tax calculated, payment method selected, shipping choice determined, rolled-up order and, finally, order confirmation communicated back to the buyer.

In buy-side procurement activities, additional steps involving approval, other workflow actions, and managing contract compliance are often introduced into this process. Various software modules assist with these processes.

Catalogues

Catalogues, and other content management systems, are used to present customers with information about goods and services offered for sale, bid, or auction. Some catalogue applications are designed to manage large numbers of individual items, and search capabilities help buyers navigate quickly to the items they want. Other applications are designed to emphasise merchandise presentation and special offers — much as a retail store is laid out to encourage impulse or add-on buying.

As with other aspects of e-business, it is important to match catalogue design and functionality to a company's business goals. Although two applications may be called e-business catalogues, one may be completely wrong for a particular company while the other may be a near-perfect match.

E-business catalogues are primarily designed to present products to potential buyers as they browse a Web site or use the site's search function. These catalogues typically provide more information about products than paper catalogues. Traditional attributes such as item number or stockkeeping unit, item description and unit price can be supplemented with related information such as a photograph of the item, sample colour swatches, product or engineering specifications, a material safety data sheet, computer-aided design drawings or a video demonstration.

Consumer catalogues may also provide information supplied by other customers (such as book or product reviews) or an opportunity to chat with other shoppers on the Web site.

Configurators

If the product being sold has simple features, few variable components and straightforward pricing, then a simple catalogue may be sufficient to store the product's attributes.

However, if the product's feature set is large, maps to a broad range of customer requirements, can be composed of many interconnected elements and is priced accordingly, then it is unlikely that a catalogue will be sufficiently flexible to model the various product lines and options.

Examples of such products include networking or telecommunications equipment, high-end servers, desktop computers, automobiles, high-performance bicycles, life insurance policies, or mutual fund investment opportunities. In the case of such products, a configurator is the foundation technology to provide the needed functionality.

A configurator is a special-purpose software tool that allows a user to define a product that meets given criteria or needs and whose features and options can be combined to work together. Configurators may also compute the price of an assembled item, calculate payments, or compare the difference between leasing and buying or between buy and repair options.

Typically, a configurator contains: a reasoning engine; a configuration model builder; an explanation facility that gives the user a context-sensitive rationale for why a choice is unavailable as well as suggestions for alternatives; and application programming interfaces (APIs) to external languages, applications, and databases.

Configuration software needs: an underlying component or product database; the necessary logic to define rules or express constraints; and programmed operations that can evaluate combinations based on rules or constraints in concert with the buyer's stated criteria.

Initially, configurators were add-on modules to back-office ERP systems and were used by trained sales specialists or as part of sales force automation tools. However, e-business promotes unassisted selling, sometimes called customer self-service, and configurators with intuitive Web interfaces are beginning to be deployed in this environment.

Commerce platforms

One set of vendor offerings for e-business, commonly referred to as commerce platforms, provides software, a framework and tools for the development of e-business capabilities.

Commerce platforms are intended primarily for mid-sized and large e-business sites that require a great deal of customisation and flexibility. These platforms make it easier to develop e-business applications such as feature-rich catalogues or ordering systems.

They provide a well defined set of APIs as well as the integration of common modules that e-business applications require, such as payment methods or shipping logistics. However, these platforms also need a high level of technical and programming expertise to implement their capabilities. Deployments are complex undertakings that require application development, integration, and maintenance.

INTEGRATION WITH ENTERPRISE SYSTEMS

Equipped with the necessary hardware, software and application tools to establish a Web presence, the business must address issues of integration with its legacy systems before it can effectively conduct business over the Internet.

Integration is critical to e-business. It is the bridge that connects an organisation's e-business systems with its pre-existing enterprise applications. This section focuses on the near-term technologies that companies will need as they begin to integrate existing information technologies with new e-business systems.

The technology candidates that will see the most activity in the near future are e-business extensions to enterprise resource planning systems, electronic data interchange, and enterprise application integration technologies. The goal of these systems is to link entire sales, production, and delivery processes and systems electronically into one seamless flow of information between an enterprise and its partners.

Integration is not a trivial undertaking, however. Organisations are discovering that e-business requires them to integrate formerly disparate systems and applications at a higher level of interactivity than before.

Approaches to carrying out the integration differ and their applicability depends on the extent to which an organisation uses e-business. The approaches roughly fall into four areas.

Custom development

The lowest-level technical response involves complete custom integration between multiple applications. The custom-developed integration would need to handle everything from the basic details of moving data reliably from one application to another, to the business logic that implements the integration of the two applications' functionality.

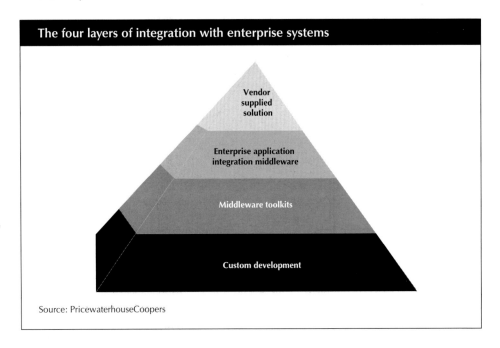

The four layers of integration with enterprise systems

Vendor
supplied
solution

Enterprise application
integration middleware

Middleware toolkits

Custom development

Source: PricewaterhouseCoopers

Middleware toolkits

The next approach relies on classic middleware. Middleware describes several different types of software, all of which sit in the middle and provide connectivity between two or more other types of software. It can also translate information between software.

Enterprise application integration middleware

EAI (enterprise application integration) is packaged middleware for connecting e-business systems with other enterprise applications. It integrates multiple applications that could otherwise not be integrated without custom software development.

EAI provides the business logic as well as the data transfer aspects of application integration. The package provides business process interfaces for typical functions such as order entry, so that a new order placed via an e-business Web site can contact and update all the applications involved in the order-entry process.

Vendor supplied solutions

In the final approach, a single application vendor provides integration between multiple components of its application suite. The result would be similar to that described for EAI middleware but without the need to buy third-party software to connect the applications.

An application vendor can typically provide integration between its own applications that is tighter and more seamless than is possible with applications from multiple vendors. This is because fewer inconsistencies must be bridged between the underlying data elements and logic of the two applications.

PERSONALISATION AND SECURITY

Unlike a broadcast mechanism such as print, television, or radio, where the entire audience or readership receives the same content, each Web user has an individual connection to the on-line presence of a business.

To take advantage of this new mechanism, instead of providing the same content for everyone, a site can provide personalised content to each user.

Personalisation involves tailoring the presentation of a site to individuals or classes of customers based on profile information, demographics, or prior interactions. The goal of personalisation is to market and sell one-to-one and to enhance the user experience and build customer loyalty so the customer returns again to the site.

User profiles

In its simplest form, personalisation is achieved through user registration. When users initially visit a site, they are asked to provide demographic information and indicate preferences or categories of interest.

The user profile information is stored in a database along with a unique user ID and password. When users revisit the site they are prompted to log in, using this ID and password, which initiates a query into the profile database and retrieves the information previously entered.

Different applications use different techniques to identify the individual. These techniques include user log in, browser cookies and personal digital certificates. Most applications today use some combination of log in and cookies, whereas digital certificates for individual users are still in the early stages of deployment.

A profile can also contain information that a user chooses to share with the system through the registration process or ongoing surveys. These methods are sometimes referred to as explicit profiling. Building profiles from transaction data about items purchased or analysis of browsing (clickstream) behaviour are examples of implicit profiling. Implicit profiling automatically tracks user behaviours and attempts to draw inferences about individual users.

Clickstream data coming into a Web site from an unknown user can be compared with patterns of clickstream behaviour from previous visitors to the site and used to guide the creation of targeted Web pages. Additionally, a data warehouse repository with this clickstream data can be analysed with data mining pattern recognition software.

This can help devise the rules that govern which message to offer the anonymous prospect, how to counter points of resistance, and when to attempt to close a sale.

Given the profile, an application can then tailor the presentation to that user. A selling application may use the profile to select special promotions to offer the buyer, such as a one-time discount, an opportunity to join an affinity programme, or the product on sale that day.

Buy-side applications can use the profile to call up previous orders to simplify purchasing the same items again.

Clearly, these profiles can be used in many other ways, especially as systems become more sophisticated. In particular, the use of profiles combined with general demographic information is becoming more common as a tool for merchandising and one-to-one marketing efforts on the Web.

Collaborative filtering

Collaborative filtering takes advantage of previous decisions made by other people with whom a given individual shares common characteristics. It can be used to select information likely to be relevant to that individual.

Collaborative filtering applications collect observations of user preferences and then make recommendations based on correlation matrices of users' tastes and preferences. This information can be collected explicitly or implicitly.

In some situations, collaborative filtering engines explicitly ask users to rate their choices. In other situations, the engines passively track the pages that users view, the products they purchase, and other choices they make. They use this information to create an implicit profile. Collaborative filtering engines then seek to predict what products individuals or groups of users will be likely to purchase, based on their similarity to other individuals and groups.

A common example is found at e-business sites selling books or music CDs. Such sites often use collaborative filtering to recommend to customers additional titles they are likely to enjoy. This recommendation comprises items selected by other customers who made the same previous purchase. The more individual information a collaborative filtering database contains, the more useful the recommendations or suggestions can be. By capturing user behaviour characteristics automatically, and so increasing the number of profile attributes without requiring users to respond to requests for information, the accuracy of collaborative filtering can be improved.

Rules-based personalisation

Unlike collaborative filtering, where the choices of previous users influence the options presented to an individual, rules-based systems match user profile data to a set of predefined rules or assumptions.

A content-matching engine is the means by which these rules are used to identify content to be received by profiled users. Several different types of rules can be applied effectively.

- A content rule may say something like, "Show all Event_announcements whose region is Midwest to anyone whose Customer_region is Midwest."
- A customer rule might say, "Include anyone whose Past_purchases includes one transaction in excess of $10,000 in the Big_spender group."
- A profiling rule might say, "If customer indicates Home_equity greater than zero, set Home_ownership = true."

Case-based personalisation

Case-based personalisation software translates user-supplied freeform text into a query that can be run against a database. This software is most often used to automate query-handling interactions.

Case-based personalisation is often found on help desks, call centres, or automated e-mail response systems. More recently, it is being deployed in e-business venues when a user is engaged in a question/answer dialogue and unsure of the exact item desired. Case-based personalisation software matches a user with a short list of products or services.

Brightware's Advice Agent for customer assistance on the Web is an example of case-based personalisation being applied to interactive e-business situations. Advice Agent provides assistance to customers by learning their needs and showing them relevant information and solutions. It uses an automated Web dialogue to provide the personalised advice and targeted content.

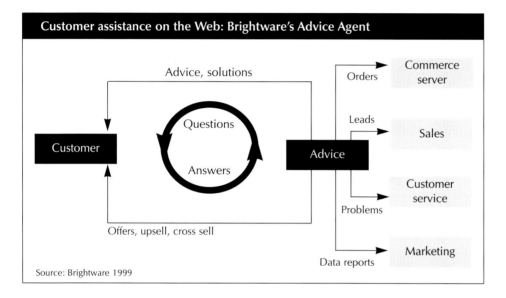

Customer assistance on the Web: Brightware's Advice Agent

Source: Brightware 1999

Security

Security technology is called upon to perform several functions in e-business transactions: authentication, confidentiality, secure delivery, privacy, and non-repudiation.

Confidentiality ensures the privacy of a transaction or message. The credit card information that authenticates a purchase over the Internet must be concealed from third parties during transmission and while in storage on the merchant sites.

Confidentiality on computer systems is normally obtained by restricting access to the data, and requiring some form of authentication for access. Confidentiality over public networks is obtained by encrypting the data.

Interest in, and use of, key cryptography continues to grow rapidly, because of its potential to facilitate electronic commerce using the Internet. In particular, it does not require an out-of-band process for secure exchange of private keys before sending encrypted messages.

Digital signatures

Digital signatures allow the receiver of a digitally signed electronic message to authenticate the sender and verify the integrity of the message. Most importantly, digital signatures are difficult to counterfeit and easy to verify, making them superior even to handwritten signatures.

A digital signature is established by creating a message digest of an electronic communication, which is then encrypted with the sender's private key using an asymmetric encryption (a public-key algorithm).

A recipient who has the sender's public key can verify that the digest was encrypted using the corresponding private key and thus determine whether the communication has been altered since the digest was generated.

Digital signatures by themselves do not provide functions such as non-repudiation. They merely prove that a given message came from the holder of a given private key — not even that the holder of the key is who they purport to be.

Proof that the signer of the message really is who they claim to be is supplied by a certification authority, which checks the credentials of the key holder before signing the holder's public key with the certification authority's certificate.

Technology trends

While this chapter presents a potentially confusing array of technical options, the task of establishing a successful e-business operation is, fortunately, made more simple by the integrated approach of the main ERP vendors.

Many of the necessary components for e-business are built into the latest versions of these systems, and businesses do not need to address each issue in isolation.

It is important to recognise that despite advances in e-commerce tools, a business will still need a backbone ERP system on which to run its operations, as the Web itself is not an appropriate environment for large-scale data storage.

Where a network of organisations is using e-commerce to share information, technology makes it feasible, as never before, to maintain knowledge of consumers and their preferences, and to maintain security of this data through the techniques discussed in this chapter.

Data security does not, however, necessarily imply legality, and with advances in technology come advances in legislation to avoid misuse. Data protection laws are being updated throughout the world and limit the potential access to, and use of, such information. This is an important consideration when developing a technology strategy.

KEY ISSUES FOR THE CEO

- What technology do you have currently?
- Does your current technology have the capability to get the most from e-business and e-SCMI?
- Do you understand what the Internet is capable of, an how it will affect your business organisation?
- Do you know what e-business technology is available and who can supply it?
- Does your business possess the right skills to select and implement the right technology successfully?
- Where are you on the road to e-trading fulfilment?

Harnessing the power of knowledge

INTRODUCTION

Knowledge management — the manipulation and sharing of information to create knowledge — is a critical component of successful e-supply chain management (e-SCM). The extended enterprise can only function when distributed knowledge is applied effectively. In turn, it is the tools and techniques of e-business which enable knowledge sharing to a previously unimaginable extent.

This chapter explores knowledge management (KM) practices and shows how they are becoming critical processes for enterprises in the 21st century. Its primary focus is to examine how effective companies develop and deploy successful knowledge management programmes.

The chapter highlights successful cases and demonstrates the value of extending knowledge management practices across the electronic supply chain. Knowledge management processes, frequently supported by e-business tools, will spread business knowledge throughout an organisation and its business partners.

This sharing of real-time knowledge among employees, partners and customers through Internet technology will have a profound impact on future businesses. The ability to learn from this new knowledge and create new products and services faster than the competition will help organisations win in this new marketplace.

Using groupware, databases, the Internet and other software tools, a growing number of businesses are trying to combine readily available explicit data with the

To set the landscape, senior management should answer 'true' or 'false' to these statements as they apply to them.
- Your organisation is a knowledge-sharing organisation.
- Sharing knowledge in your organisation is a priority.
- There are tangible signs of knowledge sharing throughout the organisation.
- Sharing knowledge across departments occurs regularly.
- Sharing knowledge with your customers is one of your business practices.
- Sharing knowledge with your trading partners is one of your business practices.
- The company regularly uses knowledge from its customers and trading partners to create and enhance new products and services.

Just one reply 'false' to any of the above questions shows that while some level of information sharing may occur in an organisation, transforming that information to create and enhance new products and services cannot always be demonstrated.

tacit information in employees' heads. Effectively, they are trying to create a knowledge base of intellectual capital.

Indeed knowledge management is now widely acknowledged as a concept worth pursuing. An April 1999 survey conducted by *InformationWeek Research* found that the majority of IT executives considered knowledge management to be of strategic importance to their businesses. They rate it as a strong 7.2 on a scale of one to 10, where 10 is extremely strategically important. Only 6% rated it as "not very important".

Many firms are signing on to the knowledge management bandwagon, but few are implementing fully functional programmes that achieve tangible business benefits. The knowledge management programmes of many well intentioned companies often consist of a quick mission statement, a state-of-the-art database and a release message!

Those businesses that have experienced success in realising the full value of knowledge management have deployed a comprehensive programme that focuses on managing business and customer knowledge. Their goals are to produce better products and services, facilitate horizontal interaction across the business, and share successful practices and lessons learned within the organisation.

In this chapter, e-business and new channels of information will be examined as to how they affect knowledge management. For companies intent on transforming their business, the active capture, analysis and leveraging of key knowledge relating to customers, suppliers and internal business must be done well.

KNOWLEDGE MANAGEMENT: A CRITICAL PROCESS FOR THE 21ST CENTURY

As new information channels again accessibility through the Internet, data management can quickly become an overwhelming process. Coupled with this are problems relating to information delay, the location of experts and access to critical knowledge, as well as inputting new knowledge capital and packaging it so it is applicable to each individual user's needs.

As businesses continue to acquire more information, they need to invest in processes that will transform the information into knowledge assets. These processes should be developed to speed innovation, enable collaborative practices within both the organisation and the extended supply chain, and to integrate enterprise wide learning.

To create successful knowledge management programmes, businesses must:

- Map their business processes and address the cultural issues in knowledge harvesting, usage, marketing and packaging processes.
- Become a knowledge sharing organisation — this involves communicating the role of all employees as knowledge workers with shared responsibilities.
- View knowledge capital as an asset that can be measured.
- Create knowledge harvesting tools and knowledge management processes that are integrated with business processes.
- Stimulate collaboration and innovation to convert knowledge capital into products, services, re-usable components and best practices.
- Relate knowledge management objectives to business goals and customer expectations.
- Enlist knowledge management resources with a mix of skills, including business and industry knowledge, technical awareness, project management skills and enthusiasm for learning.

It is not currently possible to buy an off-the-shelf solution for managing knowledge or to distribute company missives mandating knowledge sharing. This is a multi-dimensional subject that requires alignment with business strategy, organisational support and leadership, formalised and communicated sharing processes, knowledge of the employees and customers, and enabling technology.

This approach relies on several critical factors to ensure the development and deployment of an effective programme. These include:

- Understanding the value of knowledge in the organisation.
- Knowledge of the business processes.
- Leadership support.
- Integrating knowledge management into business practices.
- Reward and acknowledgement for knowledge sharing.
- Enabling technology.
- Active management of the programme.

Understanding the value of knowledge in the organisation

For some, it is easy to see the intrinsic benefits of knowledge management; a more knowledgeable work force, faster learning curves and quicker problem resolution are just a few that are frequently cited. Others will only be convinced by financial arguments such as its cost-effectiveness. This is becoming more and more critical as the stakeholders in some industries insist that a distinct value is placed on knowledge assets.

Nowadays, organisations are being evaluated not just on financial performance but also on intangible assets. Intangibles, such as the accumulated know-how and experience of employees, research and development, customer satisfaction, and the working environments collectively constitute the intellectual capital of a company. A recent survey of 275 portfolio managers, representing virtually all major types and classes of active institutional investors, revealed that investment decisions are 35% influenced by non-financial data.

Companies frequently look to associate a direct business benefit with the active management of intellectual assets. In some cases this can be relatively easy.

- Acquiring new customers as a result of demonstrating a rich knowledge base and skill set.

- Responding to customer enquiries from a knowledge base that tracks the results of previous enquiries, and ultimately improves customer satisfaction.

The application of a knowledge management programme can easily have an effect on shareholder value. The discovery of Viagra by Pfizer, the major pharmaceutical company, is a case in point. By chance, UK researchers into Viagra as a potential angina drug noticed increased male potency. However, rather than dismiss the discovery, they sought out the best suited management team in the US to take it further.

Having a good knowledge management regime in place made Viagra's discovery a certainty, not dependent on chance.

Knowledge of business processes

Capturing and re-packaging of business knowledge and thought capital should be developed in line with the way the enterprise is conducted. Too often organisations design knowledge systems according to the latest technology and buzzword solutions rather than applying an approach that reflects and codifies their business processes.

In the development of such a programme, the users of the system should contribute to its design. Developing a knowledge management programme cannot be driven solely by the IT department, it must be championed and designed by business leaders and process experts within the organisation and frequently by suppliers and customers of that organisation.

This will help ensure that the design is accepted and understood by its users and that the content is organised correctly so that it is readily available and becomes indispensable to the conduct of thier normal activities. In particular, the system must capture key data points, such as knowledge of customers, products and services, competitors, suppliers and internal capabilities.

Leadership support

The acknowledgement and endorsement of knowledge management programmes must come from the top. Unless there is a concerted effort from senior management, a knowledge-sharing organisation will not evolve.

This support can come in many ways, but a few critical ones must be incorporated:

- Knowledge management must be recognised by leaders as an activity that everyone will participate in for the good of the organisation.
- Employees must be encouraged to use the knowledge tools, participate in user communities, and contribute their information to the knowledge base.
- Clear messages must be delivered that abolish knowledge hoarding and acknowledge sharing.

Integrating knowledge management into business practices

The integration of knowledge management into business practices means that the employees become participants, not spectators or observers in the programme. To encourage this change, knowledge sharing practices must be integrated into business processes. So, as designs are drawn from R&D and research is documented by marketing, and as client profiles and buying patterns are developed by sales, appropriate practices for documenting and sharing that information must be in place.

This is not a process for librarians to manage! It is for the creators and designers of information, supplied with associated tools and processes, to turn both tacit and explicit information into useful knowledge. Knowledge sharing cannot simply support the work that is done, it must be intrinsic to it.

Reward and acknowledgement for knowledge sharing

Successful programmes tend to use a combination of stick and carrot and rarely work if coerced. For example, some organisations mandate that, as part of the career advancement guidelines, some forms of knowledge sharing must be demonstrated. This, coupled with less structured practices, such as top level recognition for new knowledge contributions, would be an ideal manner in which to develop a knowledge sharing programme.

Ultimately, if the programme is robust and users find value in the information they are receiving, they will be quick to spread the word and share their positive experiences. In the end, it becomes a self-sustaining initiative.

Enabling technology

Knowledge management programmes perform best when enabled with sophisticated and creative technology. Information sharing tools such as Lotus Notes databases and other groupware are frequently applied in this area. However technology alone will not achieve a robust knowledge solution. Conversely, even the strongest knowledge management culture that is not supported with technology will probably fail.

Where applied, technology should be designed to support business practices and should be easy to use and quick to respond with results.

Active management of the programme

Striking the right balance of skills is critical for the group that will develop the programme. Organisations that only address one dimension when enlisting their development team will find that they lack a rapport with their employees. The critical factors identified earlier as part of a successful programme must also be emulated in the selection of resources.

Business process knowledge and awareness of technology solutions are just two areas that are critical. One other key characteristic is that individuals within the team should be marketing and people orientated. These will be critical to establish this new area, one that may seem foreign to the employees.

Advertising successful knowledge sharing stories, networking at special events and looking for opportunities to leverage the tools that are created are a few ways that the messages of the programme can be promoted. The team members cannot be passive about the knowledge management programme — this approach will result in a lacklustre response from the employees.

Being over-the-top may, in some cases, result in just the right amount of communication to compel the employees to investigate further — they will want to know what all the hype is about. If people are passionate and enthused about the programme, others will want to see for themselves what knowledge management is achieving.

CASE STUDY: LESSONS LEARNED IN A MERGER — PRICEWATERHOUSECOOPERS

The value of knowledge management becomes evident when it is applied to changing circumstances. When PricewaterhouseCoopers (PwC) needed to reorganise quickly after its recent merger, there was a strong urgency to commit resources and information to developing a better knowledge system.

The new firm had twice the amount of knowledge, but found that the value to be realised lay in making the whole greater than the sum. Attention was first placed on understanding the intellectual capital that both parts brought to the new firm. With this combined understanding, the tasks were to create new knowledge and services that did not previously exist, and to quickly integrate systems and the knowledge and experience of people. The management of knowledge and the fostering of a knowledge-sharing organisation were, and continue to be, of immense importance.

Clearly, both lagacy firms had their own knowledge management techniques. The merger, however, offered an opportunity to re-think how a knowledge programme should be organised, rather than inheriting one already in place. This called for a new organisational structure for managing knowledge, new practices to create a knowledge sharing firm, new ways of integrating knowledge sharing techniques into business practices, new technology and new ways of learning from our knowledge.

The initiative produced some valuable lessons about customer involvement, committed leadership, fostering a community spirit, knowledge sharing, customer loyalty, obtaining new customers and how this all fits into the extended supply chain.

Involve customers early and often

The success of a knowledge management programme will be difficult to achieve if staff do not see it as part of their responsibility. It cannot be just the responsibility of a small group of people. Ultimately the system is designed for a customer and, in this case, there are two — PwC's clients and its consultants, who must learn from collective knowledge and deliver a best-in-class service.

To ensure that consultants realised value in the knowledge programme, their input, design and participation was a necessity. The people who use the programme should be the ones designing it. The repeated message was to keep it simple. To create an easy to use knowledge system, to have one point of contact for questions, and to package knowledge so that it is available and responsive to critical business needs.

Ensure committed and informed leadership

Leadership support and commitment was identified earlier as a critical success factor of the firm's knowledge management programme. So what form does this leadership commitment take? It can be as simple as sending out frequent messages on the value of knowledge management, with encouragement to use the programme. Or it can be more elaborate, with performance measures designed to include knowledge management. Whatever the approach, an opportunity exists to demonstrate both formal and informal measures of commitment. Here are a few examples.

Formal
- Positioning knowledge sharing objectives on the business agenda.
- Key knowledge management responsibilities assigned to senior practitioners.

- Inclusion of knowledge sharing elements in performance management and career evaluation. (Within PwC, part of the standard career model evaluates knowledge sharing activities in consultants' performance reviews. It is not a box that gets quickly checked off but rather an item that is evaluated at key milestones of a client project.)

Informal

- Setting an example. Become a user of the knowledge system.
- Acknowledge those who provide some new content or help in solving a problem or issue. This simple action encouraged many of PwC's practitioners to be regular users of the system.

Foster communities

Traditionally, some management styles discourage over-socialising at work, regarding it as time wasting. However, giving these communities a vehicle to share some of their more relevant discussions can, in some cases, result in a stream of discussion that may be spread and used within the group or with like communities.

PwC's challenge was to help a multitude of existing communities to link quickly with like groups around the globe. For example, a large manufacturing group of practitioners was linked with a list of just-in-time (JIT) specialists.

This group could then be used as champions and experts for the knowledge programme as well as serving as specialists that thousands of employees could turn to for assistance.

Having identified the need for knowledge management, it is worth imagining the strength of an organisation when employees, suppliers, customers, and partners have rapid access to, and understanding of, the knowledge capital throughout their

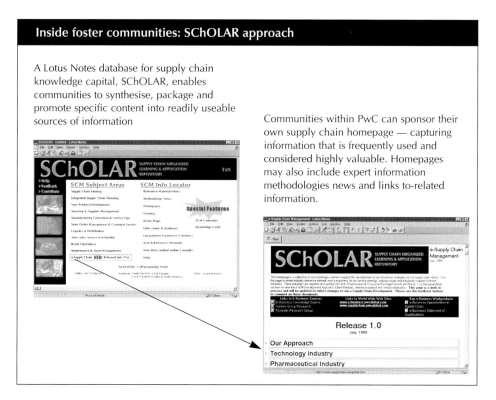

Inside foster communities: SChOLAR approach

A Lotus Notes database for supply chain knowledge capital, SChOLAR, enables communities to synthesise, package and promote specific content into readily useable sources of information

Communities within PwC can sponsor their own supply chain homepage — capturing information that is frequently used and considered highly valuable. Homepages may also include expert information methodologies news and links to-related information.

business. The organisation that can successfully manage this will have an enormous competitive advantage in the e-business arena, where speed and the ability to capture the customer's attention are vital.

E-business is helping to drive massive organisational change as structures and cultures are no longer bound by geographic, functional or even time constraints. For knowledge management this has a profound impact, as more and more unrestricted channels of information evolve.

As markets become micro-segmented, information management must serve each customer individually. When the power of e-business is harnessed to keep them up to speed, employees become more skilled and valuable to the process. With principles of knowledge sharing in place, programme and practices can be spread to trading partners and customers. The end result is that knowledge that is learned from and shared can help to create better products and services.

Knowledge sharing with consumers

By capturing, managing and responding to customer information, organisations are able to build customer loyalty and retention and obtain new customers more quickly and efficiently. Being able to capture and respond efficiently is the challenge that many organisations without knowledge management practices will face. The ability to react to this knowledge and create new, more targeted products, information and services will differentiate businesses wanting to captivate their customers.

> Yahoo!, an Internet browser and information portal, has attracted loyal customers by creating personalised space for users called My Yahoo!. This service aggregates on-line content with consumer preferences. Users can read their e-mail, design their own newsfeed, and check their portfolio, sports news, weather information and lottery results. The site allows users to change this layout, rearranging the display and making them feel that it is their own space. As a result, users stay longer at the site and return repeatedly.

Building customer loyalty and retention

By creating an information portal, businesses can address the needs of the individual. All users can see a core set of information, with buyers viewing product, price and shipping information, resellers viewing sales and inventory information, and employees viewing product development information.

Obtain new customers, cost effectively

Identifying partners throughout the business is one way that new customers can be located. Nearly every day there are mergers between complementary businesses as they attempt to provide new and combined services to a larger customer or consumer base.

This trend has been widely evident in the emerging on-line pharmaceutical delivery business. Traditional drug stores are partnering on-line stores to take advantage of their customer knowledge base. For the on-line organisation their customer know-how is attracting retailers late in the e-business game yet anxious to participate.

Similar examples exist in the on-line auto market, where Internet sources such as Autobytel and CarsDirect.com are helping to shorten the sales cycle for new cars through advanced research by consumers.

The number of people using the Internet in the US to shop for new cars jumped from 25% to 40% between 1998 and 1999. Results show that the dealer sell-through rate from customers referred by these sources averages 80%, up nearly 70% from those customers going directly to the dealership.

Leveraging supply chain partner information and creating one-stop portals that create a strong sense of community and anticipate the consumer's needs are key enablers in this process. Portals are successful when they provide targeted and specific information to communities or individuals that will drive them toward a business action. The content should change to reflect an individual's different needs.

Here are two examples where services and products are built around consumer knowledge. The first shows a high-tech company selling consumer items such as personal computers, software or components.

Business to consumer — technology	
Information and products shared by the business	**Information shared by the consumer**
• Insights on product configurations and fixes • Product FAQs, comparisons • Purchase recommendations • Upgrade releases • Customer communities, shared experiences • On-line tutorials • Developer tools	• Customer preferences and interests • Product/service value and gaps • Events that effect demand • Service issues, relationship demands • Marketing, brand strategy effectiveness • Purchase pattern frequency

Analysing customers' buying patterns, technical requests, and internal product knowledge allows the portal to deliver information that might not yet have been requested, such as related purchase information for components or communities especially helpful for developers of IT.

The second example focuses on an apparel manufacturer or retailer, that wants to provide a better shopping experience for the customer by making garment pairing suggestions, providing delivery information, or showing personalised digitised models. The meta-data will show buying selections, such as identifying that shoppers who purchased the red and green sweater also purchased khaki trousers. It will also make recommendations of supply chain partner products, such as "Would you like to view matching dress shoes for your new navy suit?"

In this example, trading partners can pair customer information with new products. Manufacturers and retailers may also form partnerships to own the entire portal. For example, shoe manufacturers, accessory retailers, casual wear retailers, business dress manufacturers and dress shirt manufacturers could now co-ordinate as a total apparel outfitter.

To improve customer management, organisations must provide content based on a

Business to consumer — apparel	
Information and products shared by the business	**Information shared by the consumer**
• On-line shopping catalogue • Wardrobe pairings based on co-ordinates/colour co-ordination and consumer purchases • Cleaning instructions • Fabric care • Digital dressing rooms • Promotion advisory based on like products and sizes • Extended supply chain: apparel suggestions and offerings from manufacturers of differing products such as shoes or accessories	• Purchase pattern frequency • Customer apparel preferences • Customer feedback • Picture scanning for personalised model creation • Size information • Other sources of on-line apparel purchases

dynamic assessment of their customer base. They must move from static information sites that push unsolicited information to portals that group and publish information based on buying patterns and customer feedback.

Organisations must have flexible knowledge management strategies that can link customer data with internal knowledge capital. The end result will be to establish a secure link with customers based on a comprehensive understanding of their preferences and needs as well as your ability to respond.

Knowledge sharing across the extended supply chain

Businesses that look across the total supply chain will provide more valuable knowledge to their customers and increase customer retention and loyalty. By providing customers with better information about products and services they can make better buying decisions and improve the experience — often leading to return customers or higher value purchases.

Pushing out that same logic to the extended supply chain, businesses need to couple this skill with the capture and sharing of the wants and buying patterns of customers throughout the organisation. If they can do this, they will find they are better able to respond to the exact needs of each customer.

Combining the knowledge of the customer, supplier and internal processes is not a new concept, rather it is now that better tools and ways to distribute the information are available. One exceptional example of the value of this partner collaboration in the development of the Linux Operating System and its relative position among today's top computer operating systems.

The original inventor of the Linux system, Linus Torvald, started with a theory of re-use when he released his version of an operating system to the Web. Linus employed what is now known as open source code — a software development process that attempts to harness the knowledge of multiple users and designers.

He invited software developers and hackers to contribute to the system by posting bugs and their respective fixes. Consequently, an operating system was created through worldwide collaboration that is endorsed by major corporations. This classic example has many of the elements defined as critical success factors:

- Reward — an individual's code designs find a permanent place in the design of the system.
- Enabling technology — a platform with which this community of users was clearly familiar and able to access globally.

Linux is renowned for its stability — something that was achieved only after thousands of developers shared the bugs they found and their recommended fixes.

It is a classic example of the old saying "two heads are better than one".

While Linux used a talent pool of thousands of users, similar approaches may be applied within an organisation or across the extended supply chain.

One practical example in which an organisation can mirror this approach is in the new product development and customer service areas. Through collaboration, products or services can be improved upon given the exchange of information from users and suppliers. Given a large enough community of collaborators, almost any product can be analysed quickly, resulting in the realisation of improvement opportunities.

KEY ISSUES FOR THE CEO

- Does your current knowledge management programme have clear strategic, organisational and business process elements?
- Is your business employing knowledge management across the entire supply chain? From your suppliers' suppliers to your end consumer?
- Is your business agile enough to respond with new products and services based on meta-data obtained from your customers?
- As a leader in your organisation do you actively acknowledge and reward users embracing knowledge sharing practices?
- Are you doing everything you can to empower your employees to be knowledge workers?

Organising for the future

INTRODUCTION

The benchmark company of the last decade is a work of great precision, rather like an automobile engine. Its functions have been painstakingly designed and can be accurately measured. This model has served most companies well. But what will happen to this organisation in the future? How will this model work when the commodity being passed around is information, not metal?

This chapter describes how new technologies will affect organisations as we know them. The future has already been glimpsed — in many companies, teleworking from home and hot desking in the office are part of the day-to-day job.

This chapter expands on these examples to outline some of the essential building blocks of future organisations.

Business organisations are, in essence, mechanisms for co-ordination that exist to guide the flow of work, materials, ideas, and money. The form they take is strongly affected by the co-ordination technologies available.

Until the 19th century, co-ordination technologies were primitive, since goods and messages had to be transported by foot, horse or sailboat. The process was slow, unreliable, and often dangerous. Since there was no efficient way of co-ordinating disparate activities, most people worked near their homes, producing products or services for their neighbours. As a consequence the business organisations that did exist — farms, shops, foundries — were usually small, without the ability to reach distant customers.

With the rapid spread of railroad tracks and telegraph lines in the 19th century, large, complex organisations became possible. Dependable communication and transportation meant that businesses could reach national and even international markets, and the owners still had the necessary means to co-ordinate and control large, dispersed groups of people. The hierarchical industrial corporation, made up of a broad array of functions and, often, a broad array of businesses, was born.

In the last few decades, there has been a rapid development in the co-ordination technologies available. Railroad and telegraph lines have long been supplemented with jet planes, faxes and mobile phones. More recently, the possibilities opened up by computer networks and the Internet have exploded beyond imagination. If improved communication and transportation led to the birth of the hierarchical, industrial organisation, what will the digital revolution lead to?

E-business will increase the speed of transactions, it will shorten the time to market, it will change the way companies work with suppliers and customers, and it will give the consumer boundless choices when it comes to products, specifications and price. All of this will be enabled and driven by the digital technology. But what will the e-business world feel like? How will we work together? Who will organise us? Who will we work for?

The organisational impacts of e-business will be significant, and they will affect our whole society. In this way, the effect of e-business will be more profound than merely ordering customised products by a mouse-click.

ORGANISATION IN REVOLT

Revolution is a word that has many connotations. For some, it conjures up a vision of quick, often brutal or violent, change. For others, it means a fundamental transformation in affairs. The notion that change must happen fast for it to be a revolution is the result of a century and a half of using the term to denote abrupt political change.

Revolutions are not always like that. The Industrial Revolution, for example, wasn't at all fast, nor did the changes in society come overnight. It spanned more than a century and was the result of many mutually reinforcing innovations leading to a large-scale re-organisation of the way people worked. When identifying a revolution, then, the emphasis should be on depth of change rather than speed.

The lessons of history

The modern organisation, the one nowadays called traditional, is relatively new. It began life around 200 years ago due to a radical change in technology. To identify the impact on organisations of the new e-business technologies, it is useful to understand the forces that brought these organisations into being in the first place.

In the 18th century, a series of inventions transformed British cotton manufacturing and gave birth to a new mode of production — the factory system. Comparable, and often related advances were made in other industries and, together, they made the Industrial Revolution.

These changes resulted in a rapid rise in productivity and income per head. They also transformed the balance of political power, revolutionised the social order and changed ways of thinking and doing.

The figure below gives an overview of some of the key technological changes that were part of the Industrial Revolution. Not mentioned are equally important advances in such areas as the iron and coal industries, clock manufacturing and water power. Nevertheless, the picture is clear. The Industrial Revolution did not happen overnight; nor did the technological advances that enabled it.

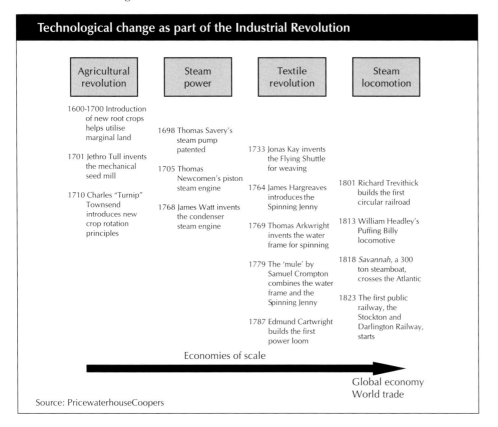

Technological change as part of the Industrial Revolution

Agricultural revolution	Steam power	Textile revolution	Steam locomotion
1600-1700 Introduction of new root crops helps utilise marginal land	1698 Thomas Savery's steam pump patented	1733 Jonas Kay invents the Flying Shuttle for weaving	1801 Richard Trevithick builds the first circular railroad
1701 Jethro Tull invents the mechanical seed mill	1705 Thomas Newcomen's piston steam engine	1764 James Hargreaves introduces the Spinning Jenny	1813 William Headley's Puffing Billy locomotive
1710 Charles "Turnip" Townsend introduces new crop rotation principles	1768 James Watt invents the condenser steam engine	1769 Thomas Arkwright invents the water frame for spinning	1818 *Savannah*, a 300 ton steamboat, crosses the Atlantic
		1779 The 'mule' by Samuel Crompton combines the water frame and the Spinning Jenny	1823 The first public railway, the Stockton and Darlington Railway, starts
		1787 Edmund Cartwright builds the first power loom	

Economies of scale

Global economy
World trade

Source: PricewaterhouseCoopers

So, what were the organisational impacts of this revolution in the textile industry?

The early textile industry was based on the concept of workers who bought raw materials from merchants and took it back to their home, where they would produce the given item. These cottage industries were competent but slow. Also, since items were produced by hand, quality varied and the workers' productivity was very low.

The merchants, though often frustrated by the lack of control over the product, did not have enough incentive to centralise the production under one roof. As long as the equipment in the factory was the same as in the cottage, factory production cost more, since workers would have to be paid a premium to leave the cottages and enter the control and supervision of the factory.

It took powered machinery to make the factory competitive. By breaking down the processes of spinning and weaving into their basic steps, it was possible to invent machines that could outperform the manual process. The steam engine provided the necessary power to make these machines larger and more efficient, and the principle of economies of scale — the dominant feature of modern organisations — was born.

And the organisational impacts? It meant the end of the small, independent cottage industries and the birth of large, hierarchical organisations — the factories. Advances in technology made it possible to standardise production and centralise control, achieving economies of scale.

However, the machinery was expensive and needed a lot of capital. As a consequence, the power of the organisation was centred round the provider of the capital, the owner. The organisation was the instrument of its owner and the individual was the instrument of the organisation. The individual was no longer an independent entrepreneur. They were a hired hand, a human resource employed to work the assets of the organisation.

As a consequence a new hierarchy of management evolved to monitor and control completion of the task.

The information revolution?

The next figure outlines some of the key technological advances seen in recent years. As in the 18th century, none of the innovations is a revolution on its own — but what of the effect of all of them together? As with the Industrial Revolution, most of the innovations have been process-improvement driven. The difference is that where innovations were once focused on improving and replacing physical processes, now they are focused on information processes.

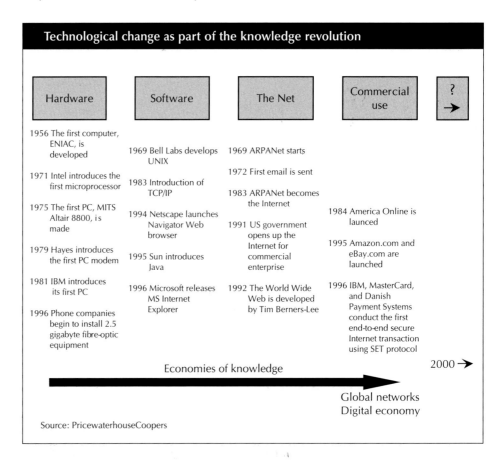

The challenge is to achieve economies of knowledge instead of economies of scale.

Why has there been this shift from economies of scale to economies of knowledge? For this one needs to start by understanding the economies of scale in large organisations:

• **Manufacture**. By imposing standards in measurement, product mix or choices on the product or service delivered, it is possible to streamline the process of manufacturing and, thereby, lower the unit costs.

- **Transactions**. The larger the organisation, the higher the number of transactions. It becomes possible to bundle transactions and make the handling more efficient.
- **Communication and control**. One only has to think of an army regiment to understand the efficiency of communication and control in a large hierarchical organisation. Information can be cascaded down the lines of command quickly, and each level can monitor and control the level below.

There are clear indications that changes in customer demands and developments in computer technologies will erode these traditional advantages.

First, customers are demanding increased product availability with greater variety and tailored solutions. Though a lot of effort is going into ensuring efficiency while producing smaller batch sizes, it is hard to retain economies of scale when customers wants individually-tailored solutions.

Second, the widespread implementation of new information technologies means that transaction costs are decreasing rapidly. In a world where transactions are completely digital, initiated with a click on a mouse, the cost of a single transaction is minimal and economies of scale are less relevant.

Finally, there has been a recent focus on the empowerment of staff. This has been helped by the ease and effectiveness with which communication can be carried out using computer networks, e-mails and video-conferencing. This greatly reduces the benefits from building large hierarchies to ensure things get communicated and carried out.

Communication reach

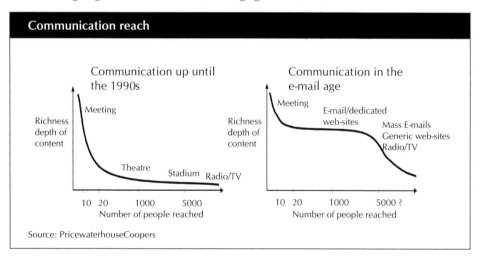

Source: PricewaterhouseCoopers

The death of the large corporation?

If economies of scale are not going to be the foundation of large organisations in the future, will large corporations as we know them disappear? The answer is that this is possible — but it is not something that will happen overnight. The existing large corporations still have reasons to maintain their size in the (near) future.

- **Access to, and knowledge of, the consumer**. This advantage, though a valid reason for maintaining an organisation, is not necessarily a long-term one. It is easy to imagine specialised marketing units selling their knowledge about consumers to the highest bidder.

- **Access to capital**. This is probably the biggest advantage for existing large corporations. Organisations with a history in the marketplace have built up trust in their ability to deliver. New companies will need to sell the idea of generating value from knowledge, with their ability to deliver being a true gamble for the investors. The capital market has a track record for evaluating risk in the traditional type of corporations. With the new, knowledge-based companies, investments will look more like a bet. Consequently the investors will demand higher returns from newcomers than from known organisations.
- **Security of payment**. Suppliers and consumers know large corporations. Suppliers trust that they will get paid and consumers trust that their order will be delivered.

Large corporations will survive for a while yet, but will the way there are organised stay the same?

THE ORGANISATION OF THE FUTURE

A survey in the spring of 1997 revealed there were 987,000 flexible workers (people working from home, or another location, and connecting to their company via telephone and modem) in the UK, equal to approximately 4% of the workforce.

British Telecom estimates that the number in 1999 is now 1.8 million and that this will grow to 4.2 million over the next five years. This trend is seen elsewhere. A European Commission report from 1998 estimated that more than 4 million Europeans at that time were teleworking — equal to 2.5% of the workforce — and that this had more than doubled in two years.

From these statistics, it is evident that many of us are already experiencing the move towards the virtual workplace. We work on portable computers, dial into the company's computer network using modems, and people often contact us on our mobile phone instead of our office contact number.

A private office in the company building is increasingly becoming a luxury that most organisations can ill afford.

Future visits to the office, may mean that one's personal space is reduced to a shelf in a cupboard and a hot desk — where the desk is shared by whoever needs it and is physically present.

An office that is available 168 hours a week but occupied for perhaps 20 is going to be a thing of the past. If there is an office in the future, it will be more like a clubhouse: a place for meeting, eating and greeting, with rooms reserved for activities, not for particular people.

From network organisation to virtual businesses

Are the changes going to stop at hot desking? It seems unlikely. Why stop at reducing the numbers of empty offices when one can get rid of the office building itself?

The example of a fashion accessories company, Topsy Tail, highlights this point. Topsy Tail has revenues of $80 million but only three employees! Furthermore, these employees never touch the products through the entire supply chain. Injection-moulding companies are contracted to manufacture the goods; design agencies are used to create the packaging; and a network of independent fulfilment houses, distributors and sales representatives distribute and sell the products.

Topsy Tail is an example of an organisation that leaves every part of the value chain to experts and just concentrates on co-ordination of the flow. This arrangement of the value chain has been called a 'network mode'.

Each node in the network is a company specialising in an area of expertise, with the business most knowledgeable about the customer controlling the flow through the network. All relations between the companies in the network are co-ordinated by mutual contracts and each company can be part of several networks.

As such, there is nothing new in network model organisations — they are just examples of fully outsourced organisations. The outsourcing of non-core processes has been common practice during the 1990s and Topsy Tail is an example where only knowledge about the customer is considered core.

There is no doubt that the near future will generate more companies like Topsy Tail. Increasing consumer demands are resulting in a focus on the flexibility to adapt quickly, and what better way to attain agility than to be in a position to simply drop a node in the network when it is no longer needed?

But why stop at networks of companies? Why not base the company itself on a loose network of people instead of a traditional management chain? The following case study, which was used in chapter 11 to demonstrate the value of information sharing, equally displays the success of such a network.

Case study: The Linux Example

Torvalds, a 21-year-old computer-science student from Helsinki, made a kernel of a computer operating system he had written available on the Internet in October 1991. The operating system was called Linux. It was a rudimentary version of Unix, the operating system that, for more than a decade, had been the backbone of corporate and academic computing. Other programmers were encouraged to download the software — for free — and use it, test it, and modify it as they saw fit.

From a slow start, the idea of downloading the code, fixing bugs, tinkering with the original code, adding new features and then re-posting the code on the Internet caught on. As the Linux kernel grew, so did the Linux community. Soon, thousands of people around the world worked on Linux, sharing their work freely with one another via the Internet.

Within three years, this loose, informal group, working without managers and connected mainly through the Internet, had turned Linux into one of the best versions of Unix ever created.

Is this the organisation of the future or just a bunch of computer programmers having fun? There are many indicators that the Linux example will be more widespread in the future.

The e-lancer at work

If one can use the marketplace to create fully outsourced organisations such as Topsy Tail, why not use the same principles with internal business processes?

To create an internal market with workers selling their skills, designers selling their ideas and managers selling their leadership, significant challenges need to be overcome in the areas of information gathering, communication, negotiation, and resolution of transactions.

In a large organisation, the costs of this have traditionally been prohibitive. As a result, decision-making is centralised and large hierarchies exist to manage the execution of work.

The introduction of powerful personal computers and the growth in Internet ubiquity, bandwidth, function, and robustness imply a change to this situation. Because information can be shared instantly and cheaply among many people in many locations, the value of centralised decision-making and expensive bureaucracies decreases.

Tasks will not be assigned and controlled through a stable chain of management but, rather, carried out autonomously by independent contractors. It is now possible for individuals to manage themselves, co-ordinating their efforts through electronic links with other independent parties.

There is no longer the need to have all the people in the same place at the same time to get work done. In fact, these people do not even need long-term contracts with any particular company.

Future organisations might not be traditional hierarchies but a confederation of entrepreneurs, united only by a common brand name. When a project needs to be undertaken, requests for proposals will be transmitted, or electronic 'wanted' advertisements posted, either internally or externally.

In this new type of organisation, the individual becomes the smallest business unit. These electronically connected freelancers — e-lancers — join together into fluid and temporary networks to produce and sell goods and services. New workers will be brought in as their particular skills are needed.

Once the project is done, the network disbands. Its members become independent agents again, seeking the next assignment.

The new co-ordination technologies enable us to return to the pre-industrial organisational model of tiny, autonomous businesses of one or a few individuals conducting transactions with one another in a market. The essential difference is that the electronic networks of the future will enable these micro-businesses to tap into the huge, global reservoirs of information, expertise, and financing previously available only to large companies.

These small companies can enjoy the benefits of big corporations without sacrificing their leanness, flexibility, and creativity.

So is it too far off to be credible? On a smaller scale it has already happened. In large organisations we see increasing numbers of ad hoc project teams, the rise of so-called 'intrapreneurs', and the formation of independent business units. The e-lancer organisation is just a couple of steps further ahead.

TRUST — THE LIFEBLOOD OF FUTURE ORGANISATIONS

In a world where every individual is a small business, how can we trust each other to deliver?

There is no reason to suppose that people worthy of their hire shouldn't go where the rewards look better. As a result, the new information-based corporations will be fragile.

If one is to enjoy the benefits of the virtual organisation, one needs to rediscover how to run organisations using trust more than on control. We will have to trust that things get done, even though we cannot monitor them.

eBay.com is the world's first and, currently, biggest person-to-person online trading community. eBay is a giant electronic marketplace selling everything from toy soldiers to cars and expensive antiques. It exists only in cyberspace, nobody can ever see or feel the things that are bought.

That means that one has to trust that the one you are dealing with actually has, say, a Louis XIV chaise to sell and that you will indeed receive the goods you have paid for. Risky? It may be, but eBay still facilitates more than a million auctions a day.

eBay.com has been successful in managing trust by creating a genuine community around its services. Members must register and provide some information about themselves before they can participate in an auction. This way, members will have a basis for building trust in one another before they engage in a deal.

Managing trust

Managing trust will be critical in an organisation that does not have a hierarchical management. Charles Handy, in the *Harvard Business Review*, describes seven principles of trust that need to be in place in future organisations.

- Trust is not blind. Those who you trust, you should know well. You should have observed them in action and share their goals.
- Trust needs boundaries. Trust, means confidence in someone's competence and commitment to a goal.
- Trust demands learning. If organisational architecture is to be made of independent and constant groupings, the groups must be flexible enough to change when needed
- Trust is tough. When trust proves misplaced, the people who let you down have to go — lack of trust leads to the introduction of checkers and controllers.
- Trust needs bonding. Self-contained units that deliver specified results are the building block of a trust-based organisation. This can create the problem of organisations within organisations. For the whole to work, the goals of the smaller units have to coincide with those of the whole.
- Trust needs touch. The more virtual an organisation becomes, the more its people need to meet in person so that people get to know each other as people.
- Trust requires leaders. Well-functioning units in trust-based organisations hardly have to be managed. They do, however, need leaders.

It is probably naïve to believe that the organisations of the future can be built on trust alone — but without trust, is seems unlikely that organisations will survive.

Facing the challenge

History tells us that non-violent revolutions take time. So, if we are indeed at the beginning of an electronic revolution, it is unlikely we have seen more than the tip of the iceberg of organisational changes.

Are companies in the future going to be anything more than a box of contracts? And is a box of contracts a sustainable basis for getting the work done in our society, or is it, in fact, a recipe for disintegration?

It is going to become difficult to hold people inside a corporation in the future. To do this, there has to be some kind of continuity and some sense of belonging. There has to be commitment — corporation to member, member to corporation.

One way of achieving commitment is to develop companies around the concept of membership. Membership of an organisation implies certain rights:

- The right to have a say in the strategy of the company.
- The right to have a veto on important issues, even including the sale or merger of the company.
- And, of course, the right to a share in the value-added of the company

Not everyone has to be a member. There can be some people with whom you enter into ordinary contractual relationships. The members are the people on whom the corporation is dependent for its long-term future. Note that commitment is not necessarily a lifetime offer — priorities and circumstances might, change and it will then be time to break up the partnership.

KEY ISSUES FOR THE CEO

- How will your organisation do business in five years time?
- What will your organisation look like if you are to be competitive in five years time?
- What do you need to set in motion now so your future organisation can take shape in time?
- In a flexible global market, how will you ensure the best people work with you and not with your competitors?

Revolution or e-volution?

INTRODUCTION

The supply chain is undergoing a 10 year revolution, brought about by the rapid, day-to-day evolution of technology. But, as in all revolutions, coming to terms with what is happening is both a challenge and an opportunity. A challenge in that the core competencies of a business continually need to be questioned. An opportunity in that resolving and reshaping them will drive the business ahead.

The supply chain revolution that is upon us brings with it a fundamental migration of value among the various capabilities within the supply chain. The capabilities in the supply chain that are strategically important and of high value today may not be the same tomorrow. So, for example, although operating systems and processors proved to be two of the most important components in the supply chain in the 1980s and 1990s, this may not be the case in the future. (And in anticipation of this, Microsoft and Intel have already been making large investments in other areas.)

The CEO's challenge now is to understand the impact of these changes and refocus the company on the new high value added capabilities of tomorrow.

SUPPLY CHAIN MANAGEMENT — THE WAY WE WERE

The supply chain of the past can generally be characterised by a high degree of vertical integration, poor collaboration among supply chain partners, and a focus on processes and cost efficiencies. The manufacturers extracted most of the value and profits from the supply chain and possessed most of the market power. Examples can be drawn from the auto industry (General Motors, Ford), the computer industry (IBM), the entertainment industry (Viacom), and the dairy industry.

For instance, in the computer industry during the 1960s and 1970s, IBM was highly vertically integrated in the mainframe computer market. It performed all functions from wafer fabrication to mainframe design. Similarly, the dairy industry was vertically integrated from farm ownership through to consumer delivery.

The traditional supply chain consisted of suppliers, manufacturers, distributors and consumers. Logistical issues needed to be co-ordinated throughout the entire supply chain, including warehousing and storage, transportation, inventory control, procurement, order processing, packaging, plant and warehouse site selection, return goods handling and customer service.

Each component in the supply chain was engaged in demand communication, or demand forecasting and co-ordination. To support these operations and logistics, IT (information technology) facilitated the flow of information from the customers all the way to the suppliers.

The main characteristics of each of the primary entities of the supply chain in the past consisted of: consumers, distributors or retailers, manufacturers and suppliers.

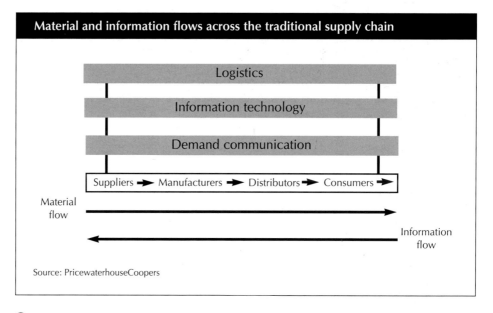

Material and information flows across the traditional supply chain

Source: PricewaterhouseCoopers

Consumers

Consumers have had little control in the buying process. They were largely influenced by mass advertising and salespeople. They were poorly informed, lacked easy access to product and price information, were less sceptical of mass marketing, and lacked alternative channels of purchase.

Distributors/retailers

The role of distributors and retailers was an important one in the supply chain, for this was the most effective means of bringing the product to the consumer. Superstores such as Barnes & Noble, Circuit City, and CompUSA generally prospered.

Case studies: finding the core competency

In effect the ultimate core competency is the ability to choose one's capabilities well. So, a company may have a core competence in certain fields — say, product design, brand marketing, custom manufacturing, or high-volume distribution — and each of these may be important capabilities in its competitive environment. However, the overriding competency is the ability to determine which of those capabilities are going to be the high value-added capabilities and which will be the commodity abilities. And, for how long?

The two examples below demonstrate that a successful enterprise will not necessarily come from the company that manages to find a great business opportunity or one that develops the best proprietary technology.

Instead success will go to companies that repeatedly can:

- Anticipate which capabilities are worth investing in and which should be outsourced.
- Determine which should be cultivated and which should be discarded.
- Analyse which will be the levers of value chain control and which will be controlled by others.

The development of the personal computer industry during its infancy illustrates this. In the 1980s, IBM launched its first personal computer. At the time, IBM was vertically integrated and dominated the computer industry. For its new PCs, however, IBM decided to employ a modular design and outsourced its operating system to Microsoft and its processor to Intel to reduce both costs and time to market.

This decision turned IBM into a commodity player in the PC industry as Intel and Microsoft extracted the majority of the value and profits in the supply chain. Today, Intel and Microsoft dominate the market through their Wintel duopoly, while IBM has, until recently, struggled to regain its once pre-eminent market position.

The car industry provides another illuminating example. The role of electronic subsystems in automobiles has evolved from an insignificant component that controlled the radio, lights, and wipers in the 1960s to one of the most important subsystems in a car today. The dollar value of the electronics in a car is overtaking that of the steel body.

Electronics are controlling many of the car's most critical systems, including acceleration, braking, steering, handling, and seating, and in the near future, the communication, information, and entertainment systems.

This shift in the automotive value chain has caused Toyota to alter its winning strategy of outsourcing many of its automotive subsystems, including virtually all of its electronic components. Recently, Toyota has begun investing in its own electronics capability.

Manufacturers

Many manufacturers were vertically integrated so as to establish a competitive advantage by controlling their supply chain and costs. For instance, in the auto industry in the US, the so-called Big Three manufactured and designed most of the important systems in the car. Only simple, low value, commodity components were outsourced. As a result, the manufacturers wielded most of the market power in the industry and reaped most of the value from the supply chain.

Suppliers

In many industries, suppliers offered parts and components that were effectively commodity products since the manufacturers were generally backwardly integrated into their market.

MARKET FORCES

A number of market forces have dramatically changed the future business environment. The two most influential have been technology, through e-business and the Internet, and globalisation.

These forces have had an important impact on the traditional supply chain, which may threaten the viability of some companies as they compete in the new business environment. To survive, these companies must redefine and refocus their businesses to leverage the migration of value in the new supply chain.

The Internet and the new e-supply chain

The Internet and e-business have had a deep and lasting impact on virtually every industry. The changes they have engendered have created both opportunities and challenges for companies as they enter the new digital era.

In some industries, these forces have conspired to revolutionise the means for distributing product; in others they have changed the delicate balance of power in the supply chain; and in still others, they are creating perfectly free markets with market demand and supply in perfect equilibrium.

In general, the Internet has created a new channel of distribution that offers a persuasive value proposition for consumers and threatens the traditional distributor and retailer.

The Internet has served as a breeding ground for virtual retailers that outsource distribution and fulfilment and focus on marketing. They offer consumers lower prices, convenience, vast product selection and, in some cases, instant delivery (software, entertainment, news, for example). As a result, virtual retailers are stealing a significant portion of market share from traditional retailers and, in the long term, may eliminate many of them entirely.

The Internet has also provided manufacturers with a compelling and effective channel to sell their products directly to consumers. Selling direct offers several benefits to manufacturers including the ability to get closer to their customers and collect valuable information on their consumers' buying behaviour.

If more manufacturers follow the lead of, say, Nike, IBM, Hewlett Packard and Sony, traditional retailers may become disintermediated from the supply chain altogether.

In addition, the explosive growth of on-line product and information services on the Internet has led to consumer empowerment — the average consumer has the ability to easily compare across vendors, peruse candid product reviews, and obtain key buyer information.

This has produced canny buyers who control the buying process with their wealth of information on prices, costs, buying terms, and products. The result is that there has been, to some degree, a commoditisation of some products, such as books and music CDs, as consumers shop for the lowest price.

Furthermore, consumers have become more sceptical of mass advertising and are more knowledgeable about products and how they compare to the competition. This places pressure on manufacturers to innovate, differentiate, and build a stronger brand identity.

The Internet also provides a venue for free market trading and purchasing of commodities through auctioning. Many utility companies and suppliers are already selling billions of dollars of product in this manner.

In the future, this model of auctioning off commodities on the Internet may also be used in other supplier markets since it benefits both suppliers and buyers. For suppliers, it allows them to be paid the fair market price for their goods and to easily sell excess capacity. For buyers, it allows the purchase of goods at their fair market value, which may offer significant savings. Examples of Internet companies that are pushing this vision forward include www.freemarkets.com, www.verticalnet.com, and www.netbuy.com.

The Internet also presents the opportunity for increased collaboration across the supply chain for the mutual benefit of all parties involved. Through such collaborative e-planning, supply chain partners can leverage the Internet to share knowledge and build long-term relationships.

This can help achieve more accurate forecasts, better integrated designs, lower costs and faster time to market for new products. This is being facilitated by leading corporate software vendors, such as i2, Manugistics and SAP, which are developing sophisticated software solutions to support it.

Globalisation

Globalisation has created highly complex processes in many industries. To reduce costs and increase efficiency and agility, many companies have begun to redesign and simplify their supply chains.

Some measures that companies are taking include vertical disintegration and increased outsourcing. They are also tending to reduce their supplier network from hundreds to only a handful that then manage sub-tier suppliers. This simplifies the supply chain and frees up cash for use in other areas.

Globalisation has also helped to fuel consolidation and vertical integration in some industries. This helps establish economies of scale and scope, provides access to new markets, and increases market coverage. According to Securities Data Corp, global mergers and acquisitions surged to a record $1.6 trillion in 1998, up 79% on the previous year.

Automotive suppliers are now being asked to design, develop, test and manufacture whole modules, while managing lower tier supplier relationships. Suppliers are rapidly consolidating and vertically integrating to meet these new demands.

This allows suppliers to take advantage of economies of scale in R&D and economies of scope in manufacturing similar components. It increases their market power, expands their geographic coverage and allows them to offer a complete solution to their customers.

THE RESPONSE TO THREATS

The information age is transforming the operating and strategic corporate environment like nothing before. It threatens to disintermediate and eliminate entire companies, supply chain links, and even whole industries. Some companies face extinction if they do not respond and evolve quickly.

The typewriter industry has already fallen to the personal computer, and computers and personal data assistants further threaten the viability of the paper organiser industry.

The critical question at hand, then, is — what is the right supply chain strategy to successfully compete in this new, precarious environment?

Of course, any successful supply chain strategy must be aligned with the overall corporate strategy, complement the marketing strategy and consider technological and globalisation issues. In addition, however, the winning strategy must encompass three fundamental competencies:

- The ability to determine which capabilities should be invested in, and which should be outsourced.
- The ability to build strong relationships with supply chain partners.
- The ability to adapt quickly and continuously.

Developing the right capabilities

In many industries, the value chain is in the middle of drastic change. Services and products that were once strategically important and high value are now being commoditised. Other services that were once unimportant are now key strategic competencies.

The e-business threat to electronic products retailing
The Internet has forced the retail industry into a revolution that is changing the fundamental economics in the industry. The exponential growth of the Internet is shifting market share, sales and value from conventional retailers. Although still in its infancy, it is becoming a formidable menace to retailing. In 1998, for example, the number of on-line shoppers grew by 300% and on-line revenues grew 200% to nearly $15 billion.

The Internet and on-line retailing have shifted value and revenues away from traditional retailers. For example, just a few years ago, retailers of electronic products such as The Good Guys, Circuit City, and CompUSA were booming. Before 1994, all of these companies experienced a high rate of growth and relatively high net margins.

Since 1994, however, the growth in revenues for these companies has dwindled. The profit margin for The Good Guys and Circuit City has also slumped as the table on the next page shows.

This reduction in revenue growth and profit margins in a mature industry is due to a number of factors, one being the rise in the sale of electronic products through the Internet. In the US alone, the on-line sale of electronic products amounted to nearly $1.2 billion in 1998. It is a clear indication that e-commerce is disintermediating traditional retail stores in this industry.

This suggests that traditional retailers need to refocus their resources to the areas in their value chain that have not been commoditised and are still high value.

It may make sense for them to realign themselves and focus primarily on providing

Company	Growth in revenues prior to 1994	Growth in revenues since 1994	Growth in revenues from 1997-1998	Net margins prior to 1994	Net margins since 1994
The Good Guys	29%	6%	4%	2.03%	-0.35
Circuit City	29%	14%	17%	2.79%	1.86%
CompUSA	58%	25%	15%	-0.13%	1.25%

electronic services, such as repairs, upgrades, installation and purchasing advice. This moves them out of being a commodity retailer selling goods at the lowest price since this strategy will not compete effectively with the on-line retailers that have lower fixed costs.

Developing the right capabilities in the cola industry

Another example that demonstrates the importance of being able to choose capabilities well can be found in the cola beverage industry during the 1980s.

In the early 1980s, the primary players in the cola industry were the concentrate producers (such as Coca-Cola and Pepsi), the bottlers (which added carbonated water and high fructose corn syrup to the concentrate before bottling the product) and the distributors (the retail stores).

At the time, Coke and Pepsi did not own the bottlers, but relied on a legacy franchise bottler system in which Coke and Pepsi granted regional bottlers the right to bottle, sell, and advertise their beverages to local retail stores.

Increased competition and globalisation during the late 1980s, however, changed the economics of the supply chain. This prompted both Coke and Pepsi to discontinue their practice of outsourcing bottling and instead bring this key competency in-house. The reasons for this change in strategy are outlined below.

Historically, the franchise bottler system provided the concentrate producers (Coca-Cola and Pepsi) many advantages:

- It allowed the concentrate producers to focus on their core competencies of product development and marketing.
- With the franchise system, although Coke and Pepsi did not own the bottling process, their supplier power allowed them to control many (although not all) important aspects of the bottling process. This included setting standards for operating procedures, pricing, marketing support, policies in bottling competitive products, and so on. As a result, Coke and Pepsi were able to enjoy much of the control that they needed in bottling without being exposed to the risks and high fixed costs of owning the bottling facilities.
- Coke and Pepsi were able to concentrate on the component of the overall value chain that yields the most value and highest margins (29% pre-tax) — producing and selling the concentrate. Since the costs in this part of the value chain are primarily variable costs, there is relatively little risk in operating in this part of the value chain. By contrast, the bottling industry is a capital intensive industry with low margins (9% pre-tax).
- The concentrate producers were able to form a flexible, decentralised network of bottlers that could quickly respond to local market needs. This was important since

it allowed bottlers to better respond to the local demand of retail stores to provide continual brand availability and maintenance.

The advent of the Cola Wars and aggressive expansion into international markets began to expose important disadvantages of the franchise bottler system. It motivated Coke and Pepsi to vertically integrate into bottling to establish cost and operational advantages.

- Economies of scale were achieved that were not possible with the fragmented franchise system. By buying and consolidating the bottling process, Coke and Pepsi could achieve lower costs, accelerated learning curve effects and better integration of operations in the overall process of producing soft drinks.

- The Cola Wars had weakened many independent bottlers, resulting in under-investment in plant and equipment and a lack of capability and time frame to effectively handle corporate goals for a given market. By acquiring these bottlers, Coke and Pepsi could better align the bottling process with their business strategy and better control the level of investment in plant and equipment to maximise production efficiency.

- In addition, the Cola Wars resulted in reduced prices and margins. In buying the bottlers, Coke and Pepsi could better control costs, a high proportion of which were in the bottling process.

- The franchise system prevented Coke and Pepsi in many instances from controlling quality and distribution, which was becoming a serious problem as they expanded internationally. As a result, this also provided an incentive for the companies to acquire some of their international bottling franchises.

Companies in this changing global environment must therefore choose their capabilities well to focus on what adds value.

A framework for capabilities development and selection

	Competitiveness Low	High
Strategic importance High	Improve or seek partner	Keep and leverage
Low	Find alternative supply	Seek differential advantage

Source: PricewaterhouseCoopers

In general, competencies that are, or will be, strategically important should not be outsourced. If the company does not own this competency, or is at a competitive disadvantage in performing it, it should reengineer the process to improve it or seek a strategic partner.

All other capabilities should be outsourced, unless the company has a competitive advantage in one of these capabilities.

Building strong relationships with supply chain partners

The second fundamental competency needed for success in the years ahead is the ability to develop strong relationships with supply chain partners. This is a major shift from previously uncoordinated supply chains.

The automobile industry
Historically, vehicle manufacturers have relied on a large number of suppliers which manufactured components to exact specifications. Car manufacturers typically had numerous suppliers for each component and selected them on price.

This approach created an adversarial relationship among competing suppliers, and between the car manufacturer and its suppliers. It led to a lack of information-sharing

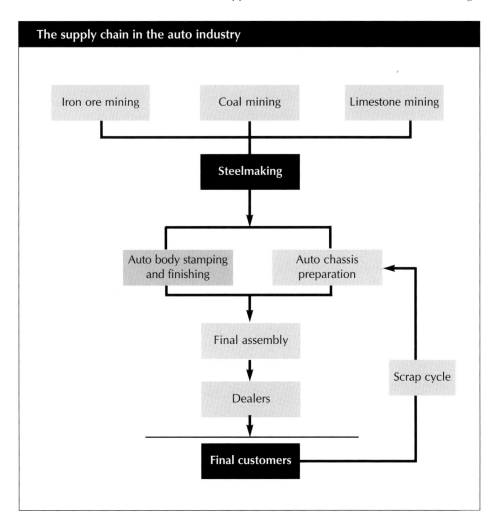

The supply chain in the auto industry

Case studies: Toyota and Chrysler

Toyota and Chrysler were the first car manufacturers to demonstrate the advantages from cultivating close relationships with their supply chain partners.

Toyota

Toyota single-sourced components from a smaller group of suppliers which were engaged in long-term contracts. In addition, Toyota would give suppliers performance specifications rather than specific design specifications.

   The result was that Toyota and its suppliers shared process knowledge, improved co-ordination, and provided incentives for innovation. This allowed Toyota to lower costs, offer new products and features, and shorten delivery time to market.

Chrysler

Because of financial problems, Chrysler was forced to redesign its supply chain in the early 1990s.

   Instead of dictating to suppliers and trying to pit them against one another, Chrysler promised to commit to long-term relationships for developing entire subsystems. At the same time, Chrysler dramatically reduced its component development and technology development activities and, as a result, the corporate overhead associated with them.

   By outsourcing the development and integration of numerous automotive subsystems, Chrysler dramatically cut the total time and cost required to develop and launch a new vehicle.

   In addition, Chrysler has been a leader in partnering with suppliers, dubbed "the extended enterprise" by Chrysler management. Chrysler shares the benefits of any cost-saving ideas with suppliers through its Score (supplier cost reduction effort) programme. In 1997 alone, this saved about $1.2 billion from Chrysler's purchasing bill.

   The company has gone from near bankruptcy to the most profitable in North America in less than a decade because of its low cost structure and its ability to charge a price premium due to cutting edge designs and features.

across organisations and created co-ordination problems in a very complex supply chain. The end result was long development times for new models (five to six years) and high costs due, among others reasons, to high inventory levels.

The retail market
During the 1980s, Wal-Mart began its now renowned practice of collecting large amounts of data on customer purchases and data mining this information to forecast demand.

   Unlike other retailers in the grocery industry, Wal-Mart shared this data with its suppliers. The result was a system of highly effective collaborative forecasting, leading to much reduced inventories and increased customer fulfilment levels.

   Collaborative relationships with supply chain partners can lead to a number of important benefits that include:

- Better integrated designs.
- Faster time to market for new products.
- Lower inventory levels.
- More accurate demand forecasts.
- Improved customer fulfilment levels.
- Lower costs.

It is also clear that the Internet and other technologies, such as certain advanced planning systems (APS), greatly help this collaboration. As an increasing number of companies continue to use e-business to collaborate better with their business partners, any company that is slow to do so will be at a competitive disadvantage.

Adapting quickly and continuously

The third core competency for effective e-supply chain management is the ability to adapt quickly and continuously.

Technology is advancing at a blistering rate, creating new opportunities and threats for businesses with each new innovation. This technology is becoming more available to a wider audience as witnessed by the continued exponential growth in Internet users and e-commerce sales. This, in turn, has spurred a number of companies to make changes to their operational and supply chain strategies.

Manufacturers such as Hewlett Packard and Sony have established an on-line presence to sell directly to consumers. Traditional retailers such as Barnes & Noble have supplemented their traditional retail sales with on-line sales to compete against the virtual bookstores. Financial institutions such as Bank of America and Discover Card have offered their customers transaction services on the Internet, including bill payment and access to account information.

In the future, as broadband and wireless technology mature, these companies will have to redefine their strategies once again. To remain competitive in this environment of rapid technological change, companies must adapt and redefine themselves at an equally fast pace. The changes that are evident have two important implications:

- Product lifecycles and product development time shortens — more competitive products are being introduced at a faster rate, forcing companies to continually adapt and change to effectively compete. Andy Grove, the chairman of Intel, once said the business model for Intel became obsolete and needed to be redefined every four years, and that this process was becoming ever shorter as the product lifecycle for processors was becoming increasingly shorter. In the automobile industry, the product development lifecycle has decreased dramatically from roughly 60 months in 1990 to only 17 in 1997.
- These increasingly shortened processes lead to mass customisation, which necessitates significant changes to the supply chain in many industries.

The overall result is that companies need to re-engineer their supply chains to enable rapid adaptability and change. They also need to continuously monitor the technological, competitive, and global landscape for changes that may hit their supply chain and act accordingly. It is also important to consider and balance trade-offs between supply chain agility and flexibility with customer service and costs.

As customer service is improved through faster (and more expensive) transportation, more efficient order processing and better stocking of inventory, then and lost sales decrease. At the same time, however, total costs fall since greater efficiency initially helps to solve severe operational problems. As efficiency is improved further, costly operational inefficiencies no longer exist, and so improved speed and customer service begin to increase total costs.

As speed and agility is increased through faster and more costly transportation methods, the inventory is reduced. The basic reason for this is that the size of the inventory buffer needed while waiting for a replenishment shipment can be smaller when the method of shipment is faster. Total costs initially fall then rise.

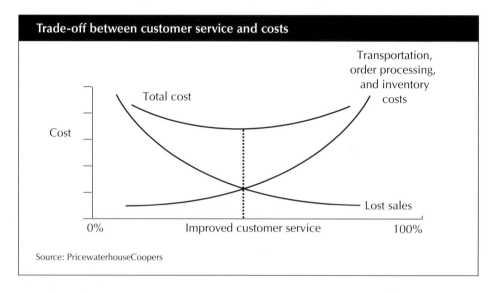

As the method of transportation is improved, dramatic savings in inventory are seen initially, which more than compensates for the increased costs in transportation (and hence total costs decrease). After a certain point, however, increasing the speed of transportation results in smaller and smaller savings in inventory levels such that the savings do not justify the increase in transportation costs.

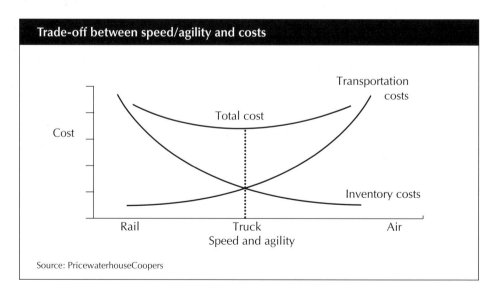

THE VISION

The supply chain has evolved significantly over the past few decades and is poised for yet another transformation, driven primarily by technology and globalisation.

The evolutionary process is converging towards a new model that embodies our prescribed recipe for a successful supply chain strategy: investing in the right capabilities; establishing collaborative relationships with supply chain partners; and, adapting quickly and continuously.

The supply chain of the past was, in general, highly vertically integrated. This made sense at the time since manufacturers needed to tightly control costs to compete and this was the only way to effectively co-ordinate the supply chain. In addition, some manufacturers were concerned that suppliers were gaining too much market power as they grew in size and threatened to steal part of the manufacturers' value in the supply chain.

As competition intensified, however, due to globalisation and the rise of niche competitors, vertically integrated companies found themselves to be at a severe disadvantage. These firms found that their large size, organisational inertia and complexity prevented them from acting with the necessary speed and agility. This has led to de-verticalisation in many industries.

This phenomenon caused some researchers in supply chain management to consider whether it is possible to achieve the benefits of vertical integration without the associated liabilities.

It now seems that e-business and the Internet offer the potential for this through the close collaborative partnerships that technology allows. So the future will bring 'extended virtual enterprises' in which supply chain partners work together as if they were vertically integrated, yet retain the flexibility and agility needed to adapt and respond quickly to changes.

E-business and the Internet offer a new era in supply chain management that will require careful selection of the capabilities that a company will own, close relationships with supply chain partners for all other needed capabilities, and the ability to adapt quickly and effectively.

We have defined e-business as the application of information technologies to facilitate the buying and selling of products, services, and information over public standards-based networks. It involves selection of the right technologies and technology providers. However, much of the initial emphasis on e-business has been on the 'e' rather than the 'business'. It is essential to remember that e-business is about the re-engineering of processes, the cultural change in management policies, performance metrics and organisational structure across and beyond the enterprise as much as it is about technology.

The e-supply chain of the future will be fraught with change and new challenges as every company in every industry is affected by the disruptive forces at hand. The stakes are high, and the rewards vast. The challenge to compete is before you. The winners will be those companies that can best leverage the new e-supply chain.

So how do the leaders of tomorrow compete in what will become a revolution through the rapid evolution of technology?

The only way to compete in the future is to define it.

KEY ISSUES FOR THE CEO

- Do you understand the impact of e-business on your company and its supply chain?
- Can you define the future for your business?
- What must you do to stay ahead of your competition?
- How are you ensuring that your business remains a part of the supply chain of the 21st century?
- What is your strategy to survive the revolution?

The growth of e-business is presently the biggest issue facing supply chain management. PricewaterhouseCoopers has a substantial pool of skilled practitioners who understand the trends and technologies in this field.

A number of our leading partners and consultants are recognised here for their contribution to the writing, editing and production of this publication. Many others have supported the thinking behind these chapters and we would like to thank all our colleagues who have contributed either directly or indirectly.

Nick Ford

Nick Ford is a director of PricewaterhouseCoopers and is one of the European procurement team within the global supply chain management practice. He is a member of the e-procurement leadership team in PricewaterhouseCoopers EMEA.

Nick has been a speaker at many conferences on strategic procurement and electronic procurement and is working with major clients to demonstrate the benefits of the firm's full value procurement approach.

Nick was responsible for chapter 9, "Sourcing for production – e-design".

Matthew Faulkner

As a partner in PricewaterhouseCoopers, Matthew Faulkner is responsible for delivering strategic change services to the west coast of the US. These services include innovation, e-business strategy and technology strategy.

David Dockray

David Dockray is PricewaterhouseCoopers' lead partner for global management consultancy services in the consumer and industrial products sector. He leads a substantial, international resource team, capable of tackling an extensive range of issues including those raised in this book.

David's supply chain expertise is recognised through his focus on delivering successful corporate transformation projects to leading international clients.

David's support for the message of this book is reflected in his introductory letter.

Matthew has assisted companies develop and implement market entry strategies, improve new product introduction processes, establish demand driven supply chain management and create business management systems to enable rapid change. His work has taken him around the world including Europe, US, Latin America and Australia.

Matthew was responsible for chapter 13, "Revolution or e-volution?".

Rob Garratt

Rob Garratt is a consultant in the supply chain management practice. His client work has included process improvement projects across a range of industries.

Before his consultancy career, Rob worked in manufacturing organisations where his management roles covered product development, marketing and information systems activities.

Rob has played a large part in the editing and production of the book, leading the marketing activities, and has compiled chapter 10, "E-essentials – the technology that drives the change".

John Kamauff

Dr John Kamauff is a partner in PricewaterhouseCoopers' management consulting practice. Before joining the firm, he led his own international management consulting company for 14 years

and has nearly 20 years' experience in a variety of consulting and management positions for leading commercial concerns. In addition, he has taught operations management in the US, Canada, Germany, Mexico and Ecuador, and has written numerous teaching and research cases.

John was responsible for chapter 1, "The challenge".

Andrew Jackson

Andrew Jackson is a director in PricewaterhouseCoopers and has over 10 years' consulting experience in Europe, North America and Asia. He has a specialist knowledge of supply chain planning processes.

Andrew's experience of large implementations of technology solutions has helped clients maximise the value from ERP implementations.

He has expert knowledge of advanced planning and scheduling (APS) tools and has successfully implemented APS programmes for the firm's leading clients.

Andrew was responsible for chapter 7, "Creating virtual advantage – planning the optimised supply chain".

Melissa Marroso

Melissa Marroso is a manager in the firm's supply chain management practice. She has combined her knowledge of supply chain management, e-business and knowledge management to advise organisations in the transportation services, automotive, pharmaceuticals, and consumer packaged goods industries.

Melissa is responsible for the global management and direction of PricewaterhouseCoopers' supply chain knowledge management programme.

Melissa was responsible for chapter 11, "Harnessing the power of knowledge".

Nick Miller

Nick Miller is a manager in the supply chain management practice. He has over 16 years' consulting experience and has particular expertise in computer modelling of supply chain and stock control systems, aimed at optimising costs and service levels. His assignments have covered all aspects of the supply chain and he has worked with several leading retailers to prepare them for future optimisation and growth.

Nick was responsible for chapter 4, "Selling in cyberspace – the brave new world of retailing".

Conrad Nowikow

Dr Conrad Nowikow is a director in PricewaterhouseCoopers and has over 20 years' experience in the application of information technology across a wide range of industries. Over the last four years he has defined electronic commerce strategies for major banking, telecommunications, IT and media organisations.

Conrad is one of the European procurement team within the global supply chain management practice. He is currently a member of the e-procurement leadership team in PricewaterhouseCoopers EMEA.

Conrad was responsible for chapter 8, "Sourcing for support – e-procurement".

Jan Paulli

Jan Paulli is a consultant in the firm's supply chain management practice.

His client work has included process improvement projects across a range of industries, and development work on computerised decision support systems for distribution planning.

Before his consultancy career, Jan worked at the University of Aarhus in Denmark, lecturing and researching in the area of supply chain efficiency improvements.

Jan has made significant contributions to chapter 2, "The future in chains – the view from the bridge" and chapter 12, "Organising for the future".

Ray Powell

Ray Powell is an industry expert in logistics and distribution, with consultancy experience covering a variety of supply chain strategy and operational improvement assignments.

Ray has worked for blue chip clients in a range of industry sectors including FMCG (manufacturing and retail) hi-tech, apparel and financial services.

Before joining PricewaterhouseCoopers, Ray spent eight years with one of the UK's leading logistics service providers, where he held a number of senior management positions.

Ray was responsible for chapter 6, "Living with the enemy – working with service partners".

Richard Powell

Richard is a manager in the firm's supply chain management practice.

He has led assignments across the breadth of the supply chain, at both the strategic and operational levels, and in most sectors. Before joining PricewaterhouseCoopers, Richard undertook a range of line management roles for a global logistics service provider.

Richard managed the production of the book, leading the editing and distribution activities, and was responsible for the executive summary.

Jeremy Robinson

Jeremy is a member of the European procurement team within the firm's supply chain management practice. As a consultant, he has worked in several industry sectors, including retail, home shopping, utilities, cosmetics, entertainment and media.

He has also spent over 11 years in line roles in the manufacturing sector in R&D, operations management and procurement.

Jeremy has been a key part of the editing team for this book.

Jim Tizzard

Jim Tizzard has operations experience covering a range of industry sectors including chemical, pharmaceutical, automotive, aerospace and petrochemical.

Jim leads programmes to improve the competitiveness and financial performance of manufacturing organisations. He develops and applies innovative manufacturing solutions, working with clients at all levels, from the shop-floor to the boardroom.

Before joining PricewaterhouseCoopers, Jim spent six years with the Lucus Industries.

Jim was responsible for chapter 5, "Acting with agility – creating the e-factory".

Alan Waller

Alan Waller is a supply chain partner in PricewaterhouseCoopers and director of the Cranfield Centre for Logistics and Transportation.

Following a number of years in production line management and management services, Alan has spent the last 25 years consulting on global logistics and supply chain assignments. He has been active in the education and training of logistics professionals and has also held lecturing posts in Leicester and Warwick Business Schools.

Alan developed the material for chapter 2, "The future in chains – the view from the bridge" and contributed significantly to chapter 6, "Living with the enemy – working with service partners".

James Warner

James Warner is a partner in PricewaterhouseCoopers and the firm's global leader of supply chain management consultancy services.

His client work has focused around the areas of supply chain strategy and infrastructure; supply chain integration; purchasing and supply management.

Before moving into consultancy, James spent 12 years in line management roles covering industrial engineering, manufacturing, logistics and purchasing within British Leyland and Mars.

James has contributed to all aspects of the development of this book and has provided the global sponsorship.

Mark Yeomans

Mark Yeomans is a partner in PricewaterhouseCoopers' supply chain management practice and has experience across a wide spectrum of client initiatives including international logistics strategy, systems design and implementation, operational improvement and strategy implementation.

He has recently worked with a number of blue chip organisations to design leading edge solutions for virtual supply chains and e-commerce.

Mark has been the executive editor of the book and was responsible for chapter 2 "The future in chains – the view from the bridge" and chapter 12 "Organising for the future".

Marketing team

Carolyn Morgan, Liza Chadwick, William Ristoff and Mark Mullings from the marketing and design team were involved in the production and promotion of this book.

With special thanks to:
Andy Banks, Alex Beavers, Ruud Bos, Stephen Bradley, Johan Cilliers, Vince Colabello, David Collins, Remco Dodde, Adrian Edwards, John Gee, Marion Hall, Charlie Hawker, Jim Holec, Robert Hope, Chris Huckle, Jeff Johnson, John Levis, François Moskovici, Khoi Nguyen, Mary-Sue Rogers, Kate Sadeg, John Sewell, Sachin Shah, Rod Street, Colin Streater and Paddy Walker.

Extended thanks to Jane, Sam and Jack Powell; Alison and James Garratt; Angie Robinson; and Barbara, James and Anna Yoemans.